Making Things for Your Home

Making Things for Your Home

by Valerie Janitch

Octopus Books

First published 1973 by
Octopus Books Limited
59 Grosvenor Street, London W 1

ISBN 0 7064 0285 5

© 1973 Octopus Books Limited
Distributed in USA by
Crescent Books
a division of Crown Publishers Inc
419 Park Avenue South
New York, N.Y. 10016

Distributed in Australia by
Rigby Limited
30 North Terrace, Kent Town
Adelaide, South Australia 5067

Produced by Mandarin Publishers
Limited 14 Westlands Road, Quarry Bay,
Hong Kong
Printed in Hong Kong

The author would like to thank the
following companies for their kind
assistance in the preparation of this book:
Copydex Ltd – fabric adhesive
Cosmic Crayon Co – Finart wax crayons
Harbutt's – Plasticine and Plastone
Sellotape Ltd – adhesives and tapes
W H Smith & Son Ltd – stationery
and art materials
F W Woolworth & Co Ltd

Frontispiece:
Flower shower

Photographs by
Gover Grey Photography Limited

Contents

Foreword

This book is intended for everyone who either has a home – or is making a home, whether in a mansion or in a one room apartment. Remembering that a house needs to reflect the personality of its occupants before it assumes the character and charm of a home, I have added to each room those little personal touches which show imagination, originality and good taste. It is these finishing touches which sometimes create extra expense for the home maker and have to be postponed. Even in the most comfortable of established homes one wants to make small changes, but is deterred by the exorbitant prices of so-called 'luxury items'. And if you are not thinking of making things for your own home, but as presents for friends – or to raise money for good causes – basically inexpensive ideas are what everyone wants.

All the ideas in this book can be adapted to reflect your own individual personality and that of your home. The more obvious furnishings – cushions, tablecloths, bedspreads – have been avoided in favour of more original items, and the decorative ideas in this book can be easily adapted to these basic soft furnishings. Here then, are my suggestions: vary them as you will – but I hope you enjoy making them – and that you find the results both creatively satisfying and enthusiastically admired. I have tried always to be practical, and to appeal to everyone's tastes – feminine and pretty for the lady of the house, or perhaps her growing daughter, more sophisticated for the menfolk and with plenty of cheerful items to attract children. And if much of my work tends to have a feeling of Victoriana, we have to remember that the Victorians considered home-making an essential art. Unfortunately, this usually meant you could not see the home for furniture and bric-à-brac, but their honest aim was summed up in the legend cross-stitched into samplers by so many patient fingers – 'Home Sweet Home'.

Valerie Janitch

Introduction

People who have never made anything
before should feel they can tackle
anything in this book: all the designs are
basically simple, and easy to make from
readily available materials.
For the new homemaker, the directions
have been made especially clear and
explicit and may perhaps seem too
detailed for those with experience.
These readers can skip those bits they
consider so obvious as to be unnecessary!
The criterion of every design is to show
the reader the secrets of a professional
finish; the things you make yourself can
often look better than their expensive
counterparts in the shops.

There are very few basic essentials. Most of the remainder come in handy occasionally and perfectly good substitutes can be found around the house.

Scissors: You will need a good pair of cutting-out scissors, plus two small pairs, if possible, so that you can keep one specially for fine sewing and embroidery, and use the other for cutting paper and other jobs which require small, pointed blades.

Sewing Equipment: Pins, needles, thimble, thread . . . and a block of beeswax. This latter might sound a bit old-fashioned, but some of the old ideas are often the best, and drawing your thread through wax really does prevent it breaking and knotting.

A sharp craft knife: This is essential. The best kind has a long blade which snaps off in tiny bits, so that you can keep renewing the tip. It is well worth paying a little extra for a knife with a self-locking device to prevent the blade slipping.

Metal-edged rule: This is necessary for cutting against with the blade of a knife.

A pair of compasses: These are very useful for drawing patterns. They need not be expensive as long as they are accurate, and not too stiff to use.

A set square (T-square)*:* This does ensure complete accuracy in drawing out patterns. Alternatively, an absolutely square piece of cardboard will do.

Adhesives: It is vital to use the right one. *Fabric adhesive* sticks many more materials than the name implies. It is clean, quick-drying and reliable. *Clear all-purpose adhesive* gives a stronger bond, and is necessary when fabric adhesive is not strong enough. *Wallpaper paste* can be very useful for certain jobs: it spreads easily and does not leave a mark. Mix it a little stiffer than directed for paperhanging. *Dry stick adhesive* is by no means essential, and is expensive to use for everything. Occasionally it is very useful however and is worth having to hand. Tough, *woven fabric tape* in a variety of colours is invaluable and if you have never encountered *double-sided tape* before, you will be amazed at its versatility!

Hall

The first impression guests have of your home is when they walk through the hall. So make this room as attractive as possible.

Create a subtle, flattering light with the paper lampshade. To brighten a dull corner, arrange some colourful paper asters in a pretty vase. For a desk or telephone table, make the elegant set of table lamp, jotter and waste-paper bin in an attractive fabric.

Gold-Embossed Desk Set

A sophisticated set for a desk or telephone table. Simple lines and a strong, bold choice of covering are designed to have distinct masculine appeal – but if you use the same fabric as for your curtains or covers, you'll have a truly individual set stamped with your own personality.

Method

To make the *lampshade*:
Measure round the outer edge of one ring and add 1 inch. Cut a piece of bonded parchment this length by 7½ inches. If necessary, adjust the depth to suit the pattern of fabric being used. Cut a strip of fabric ½ inch longer than the length of parchment and to the same depth. Iron the fabric on to the parchment, overlapping ½ inch at one end, making sure it has adhered firmly all over.
Using double thread oversew one edge of the fabric-covered parchment all round one ring; do not finish stitchng the overlap. Oversew the other edge round the second ring. Stick the overlap with double-sided tape or fabric adhesive, and finish the stitching at top and bottom.
Stick braid round the top and bottom edges as illustrated.

To cover the *waste-paper bin*, measure round the outside of the bin and add 1 inch. Then cut a strip of fabric this length by the depth of the bin. Stick smoothly round bin and join overlap with double-sided tape or fabric adhesive.
Stick wide braid round the top of the shade and narrow braid round the bottom, as illustrated.

Materials

¾ yard of 36 inch wide non-fraying fabric
2 × 8 inch diameter lampshade rings, one with
   inner lamp fitting
Bonded lampshade parchment
Cylindrical metal waste-paper bin (about
   7 inches in diameter and 8¼ inches high)
A jotting pad (about 6½ inches by 5 inches)
Heavy cardboard
1½ yards of ⅜ inch wide gilt braid for the
   lampshade
¾ yard of ⅞ inch wide gilt braid
¾ yard narrow gilt braid
Fabric adhesive
Strong adhesive tape
Double-sided tape
The instructions given are for the articles illustrated but the directions can easily be adapted to different measurements to make the items larger or smaller.

Gold-embossed desk set

10

To make the *jotter*, cut two pieces of heavy card $\frac{1}{2}$ inch wider than the jotter pad and about $\frac{3}{8}$ inch deeper. Also cut a narrow strip to the same width and about $\frac{1}{8}$ inch deeper than the spine of the pad.
Place these three pieces together touching each other, (as diagram 1).
Stick tape over the two joins (indicated by broken lines).
Cut a piece of fabric $\frac{3}{4}$ inch larger all round than the card. Mitre lower corners by cutting away a triangle (as diagram 2), and slash at centre joins. Cover the outside of the card in three stages, beginning with the lower section, by bringing the surplus fabric round to the inside and sticking smoothly: fold over at centre so that the fabric is stretched round the spine, then mitre remaining corners and stick surplus fabric round as before. Finally, stick fabric inside the spine. Cut another piece of fabric fractionally smaller than the cover, and stick to the inside.
Stick back of pad to inside back of cover.

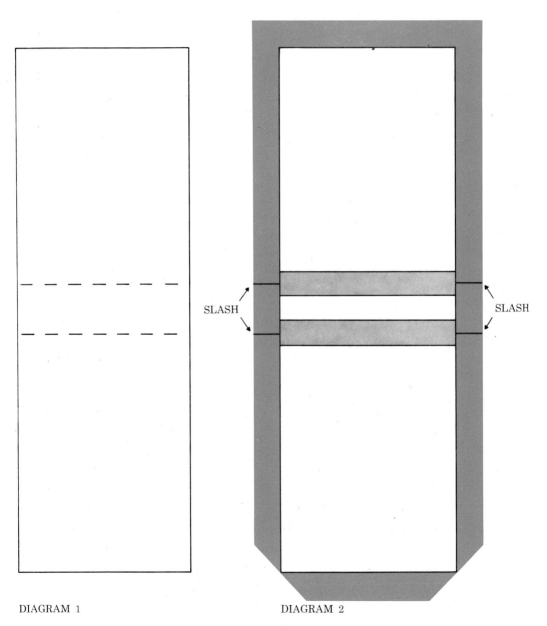

SLASH

SLASH

DIAGRAM 1

DIAGRAM 2

Green cut Paper Lampshade

This sophisticated hanging lampshade is perfectly designed for those areas where a subdued downward light is required – in hallways for instance or over a side table. The fascinating three-dimensional effect is very easy to do. All you need is a sharp knife, a metal-edged rule – and a steady hand!

Method

Cut a piece of the squared paper 7¾ inches deep by 18 inches long. Starting ½ inch from the top edge, and ½ inch in from the side, draw the top row of 10 hexagon shapes right across the paper, following the diagram. Draw seven rows of 10 shapes in this manner. The second row of hexagons starts 1¼ inches in from the side and ¼ inch down (see diagram).
Cut a piece of cartridge (construction) paper to the same size as the squared paper. Pin the squared paper over the cartridge (construction) paper securely. Prick through the squared paper, marking the ends of the solid lines. There will be six prick marks for each hexagon shape. Remove the squared paper and begin to cut and score each shape firmly and accurately (see diagram 2). Using a sharp pointed blade, and the tip of a blunt knife, cut the 4 solid lines of each shape and score the 3 broken lines. Curve the cartridge (construction) paper round – rather more than it will be when made up and gently push all the little 'windows' in. Oversew the top and bottom edges of the lampshade to the rings. Trim the overlap and stick the join. Finish off by sticking a ¾ inch deep collar of paper round the top and bottom of the lampshade to cover the oversewing stitches.

Materials

Coloured, heavy cartridge (construction) paper
2 × 5 inch diameter lampshade rings, one with inner lamp fitting
¼ inch squared paper
All-purpose adhesive
Sharp-bladed knife

Green-cut paper lampshade

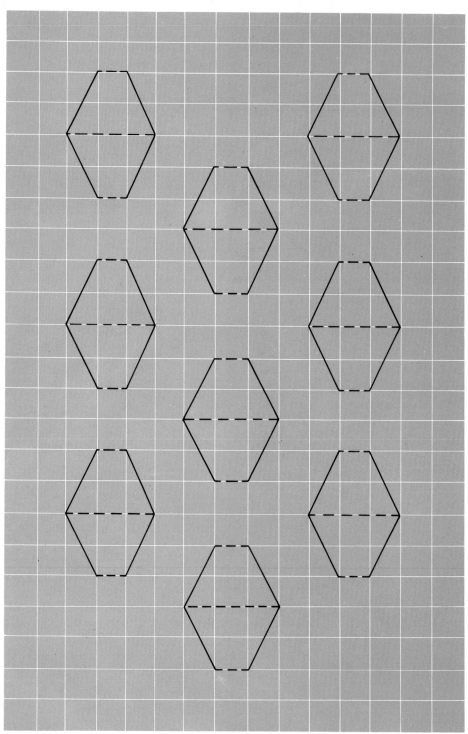

DIAGRAM 2

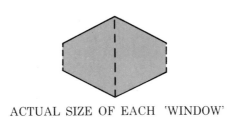

ACTUAL SIZE OF EACH 'WINDOW'

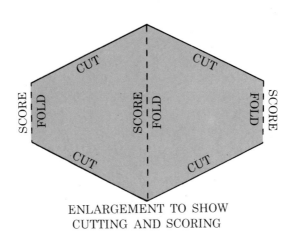

ENLARGEMENT TO SHOW
CUTTING AND SCORING

All-The-Year Asters

Shade your gathering of larger-than-life asters from delicate pink through mauve, to deep purple. Just look at a summer flower bed for colour inspiration.

Method

Hook over the tip of a length of florists' wire and wrap a scrap of cotton wool round it, moulding it into a firm ball a little bigger than a large pea. Cut a 3 inch diameter circle of bright green crepe paper, place it centrally over the cotton wool, bring the edges down all round, and secure tightly with fine wire or thread (diagram 1).
Cut two 9 inch long strips, 3 inches wide, in yellow crepe with grain widthways (diagram 2). Fold in half lengthways, as indicated by broken line. Cut a close ¼ inch deep fringe, along the folded edge of each piece, open out, turn over, and re-fold along the line of the previous fold – but do not crease. Stick the two strips together along the lower edge, then wind the double strip round and round the green centre – the cut edges level with it – sticking along the base.
Cut two 12 inch long strips, 3 inches wide, for the petals, grain as shown by arrows (diagram 3). Cut each piece down to within ¼ inch of the lower edge all the way along to form a fringe. Stick strips together along the lower edge, as before. Wind this double strip round and round the centre, keeping absolutely level and sticking the lower edge of the petals ¼ inch above the lower edge of the yellow.
Fix a garden stake to the wire with adhesive tape, for the stem.
Trace the large and small leaf patterns, following the black and coloured lines

Materials

Crepe paper in different shades – bright green, deep leaf green, yellow and pink, mauve etc. for petals
Florists' wire
18 inch long thin garden stakes
Cotton wool
Fine wire or thread
Adhesive tape
Fabric adhesive

All-the-year asters

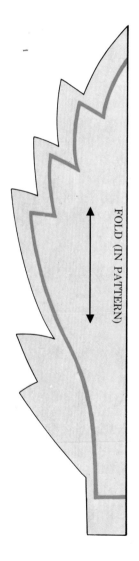

FOLD (IN PATTERN)

respectively. Cut two large and three small shapes in leaf green (grain as arrows).

Cut an 18 inch long strip, $\frac{1}{2}$ inch wide in green crepe with the grain running across. Stick one end round the base of the petals, wind round once, and then bind in the bases of the three small leaves evenly round the flower, securing with a little adhesive. Continue to wrap the strip round the base of the flower, then slowly twist it round and down the stem – binding in the two large leaves as you go. Secure the end of the strip with tape.

Open out the petals and curl gently, but firmly, stroking them between the ball of your thumb and blade of your scissors – or a blunt knife. Curl the leaves slightly in the same way.

1

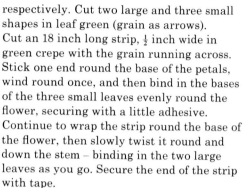

9 ins

3 ins

2

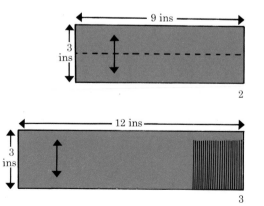

12 ins

3 ins

3

Living Room

Decorative touches add character to this room. For the walls, you can make the straw-daisy plaque or harvest trio, both of which feature dried flowers.

Smarten up a writing-pad by making a soft velvet case for it. Cover matchboxes and arrange them in interesting shapes. And, to keep happy memories, make a Victorian photograph album or a frame for individual photographs.

The coffee and cream coasters both look attractive and protect your table from unsightly rings.

Victorian Family Photograph Album

Make a truly personal photograph album to hold happy family memories. Moiré was used for the album which is illustrated, but almost any fabric can be used, plain or patterned, trimmed with lace or embroidered braid.

Method

Measure the album leaves and add 1 inch to each measurement. Cut two pieces of heavy cardboard to these dimensions. Place a leaf centrally on one piece of cardboard, and mark the position of the holes. Punch holes in the cardboard, then mark and punch corresponding holes in the second piece of cardboard. Score the inside of the front cover piece of cardboard only, to correspond with the leaves, so that the cover opens easily. Stick wadding to the outside of each piece of cardboard and trim the edges neatly. Place each piece of cardboard, wadding down, on the wrong side of the fabric; cut fabric 1½ inches larger than the measurements of cardboard. Mitre the corners by cutting away a triangle (diagram 1), and fold the edges neatly over to the inside and stick. Neaten corners with adhesive tape (diagram 2). Cut pieces of fabric 1 inch smaller than the covers all round and stick neatly to inside, covering raw edges of outer covering fabric. Pierce holes through covering, then assemble leaves between covers, fixing with ribbon or cord tied at the back. Stick trimming round the edges of the front to form a frame, using clear or fabric adhesive. Make a mock bow of velvet ribbon to trim the corner as illustrated.

Materials

Refill photo album leaves
Fabric for the cover
Wadding
Gilt or an alternative trimming
½ yard narrow ribbon or cord
¼ yard narrow velvet ribbon
Heavy cardboard
White adhesive tape (or to match fabric)
Fabric adhesive
Double-sided tape or clear all-purpose adhesive

DIAGRAM 1

DIAGRAM 2

For the living room: photograph album, photograph frame, random-shaded lampshade, wall plaque, harvest trio

22

Oval Velvet Photograph Frame

With its distinctly Victorian air, this padded velvet frame will make an elegant setting for your favourite pictures. Choose a glowing shade of velvet to tone with the colour scheme of your room.

Drawing an accurate oval is very difficult – unless you know the secret. Here is how it is done. Follow the instructions to learn the process, then adjust the measurements to make larger or smaller frames.

Materials

A piece of velvet 9 inches deep by 6 inches wide
Stiff cardboard
Wadding
Clear plastic or acetate (optional)
Fabric adhesive
A pair of compasses
Ruler

Method

Begin by drawing the inner oval (diagram 1) on your cardboard. Rule a 4-inch vertical line (A–B) in the centre of the card. Mark the centre (C) and then quarters (D and D). With compasses point on centre D, draw 2-inch diameter circles. With centre C, rule E–F 2 inches long, at right angles to A–B. With centre E and radius $2\frac{3}{8}$ inches, draw arc G–G. With centre F, draw a similar arc, H–H.

To draw the outer oval (diagram 2), mark points J $\frac{1}{4}$ inch from A and B on your inner oval. With centre J, draw $3\frac{1}{2}$-inch diameter circles. With centre C, rule K–L (through E–F), $3\frac{1}{2}$ inches long, at right angles to A–B. With centre K and radius $4\frac{1}{4}$ inches, draw arc M–M. With centre L, draw a similar arc, N–N.

Cut round the outer oval, then carefully cut out the inner oval. Place the larger oval frame on a piece of cardboard for the back of the frame and draw round both ovals (it is only necessary to mark the inner oval if you want to be able to remove the photograph. If you wish it to remain in the frame permanently, ignore diagram 3 and the accompanying directions for cutting a back

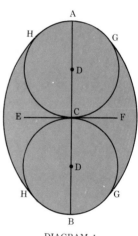

DIAGRAM 1

opening).

Cut round the outer edge of the back, but do not cut the inner oval. To make the back opening, 'frame' the marked inner oval as diagram 3. Mark centre of oval O. With centre O, rule P–Q 4½ inches long, and R–S, 3¼ inches long. With centres P, Q, R and S, rule lines, each 1½ inches long. Then join the ends as shown. Cut this shape out carefully with a sharp knife, and put to one side. Stick a piece of wadding to the front oval frame, trimming level with the edges of the inner and outer ovals. Place the front, wadding down, on the wrong side of the velvet, brushing with a little adhesive to hold it in place. Cut out the inner oval, ½ inch inside the edge of the cardboard to allow ½ inch turning. Snip this surplus velvet all the way round, to form tiny tabs. Bring these smoothly up, one by one, and stick to the back of the frame. Cut round the outer oval, ¾ inch outside the edge of the cardboard. Stick transparent plastic or acetate to the back of the frame, if required to protect the picture. If you do not wish to remove the photograph, stick this, too, into position. Now stick the back oval to the front frame. Snip the surplus velvet into tabs as before, and stick them round the outer edge of the back. If you have made a back opening, cut your photograph to size and fit into the opening, then replace the cardboard shape. Cut a piece of paper slightly smaller than the frame and stick over the back. (To remove photograph, cut round back opening with a knife and replace by sticking a slightly larger piece of paper over it, or using adhesive tape.)

Cut a 6-inch long strut, as diagram 4. Score broken line at top, and stick to back so that the frame stands at the correct angle.

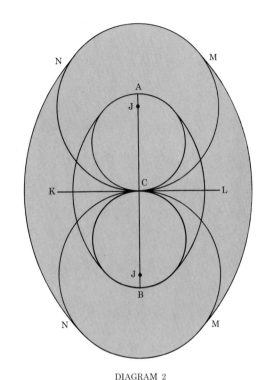

DIAGRAM 2

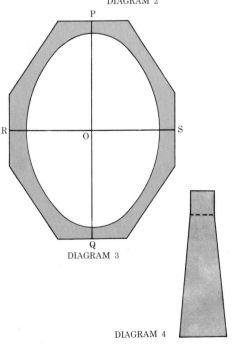

DIAGRAM 3

DIAGRAM 4

Harvest Trio

A charming set of miniatures inspired by the sun-ripened fields at harvest-time – quick and easy to make and sure to attract compliments.

Method

Cut a barley head about 4 inches long, trimming away the 'whiskers' at the top. Cut sprays of oats and heavy grass slightly longer. Tie the stalks together in a bunch with raffia.

Stick the spray to a coaster diagonally, across the grain of the wood, using either double-sided tape or clear adhesive, spreading out the heads attractively. Trim the stalks neatly.

Decorate all three mats in a similar way, to make up a set. Fix picture hangers to the backs of the mats ensuring they are positioned so that the plaques will hang at the correct angle.

Materials

3 round wooden coaster mats (about 4 inches diameter)
Wheat or barley heads, oats and grasses or other dried plants
Natural raffia or matching thread
3 self-adhesive picture hangers
Double-sided tape or all-purpose clear adhesive

Straw-daisy wall plaque and harvest miniatures

Straw-Daisy Wall Plaque

This unusual wall decoration really could
not be simpler to make. Choose an attractive
basketwork table mat and some everlasting
or dried flowers. If you do not grow
everlasting flowers (helichrysums) yourself,
then any colourful dried flowers would be as
attractive. Florists are now stocking more
and more varieties as the popularity of this
form of decoration grows.

Materials

A round woven straw table mat (about
    7–8 inches diameter)
Everlasting (dried) flowers
Self-adhesive picture hanger
Clear all-purpose adhesive
Tiny pins

Method

Fix the picture hanger to the back of the
mat, marking the front to show the way the
mat will hang.
Arrange the flower-heads on the mat, moving
them around until a satisfactory
composition has been achieved. Alternate
light and dark flowers so that they contrast
and complement each other.
Stick the flowers into position one at a time,
using plenty of adhesive, and anchoring each
head to the mat with one or two tiny pins,
driven through the petals at an angle, the
heads pushed down until they are out of
sight.

Random Shaded Wool Lampshade

The subtle colour combinations available in the range of random shaded knitting wools (yarn) can be used to great effect on many things other than knitted garments. This simple, but attractive lampshade, for example, is just a matter of winding the wool (yarn) round and round the rings – let the colours do the rest.

Method

Measure round the outer edge of one ring and add 1 inch. Cut a strip of covering material this length by the depth required. Using double thread, oversew one long edge of the parchment round one ring: do not finish stitching overlap. Oversew the other edge to the second ring. Trim the overlap, if necessary and stick the join neatly. Finish the stitching at top and bottom.
Hold a tape measure round the top edge of the lampshade and mark every $\frac{1}{4}$ inch. Repeat round the lower edge.
Secure one end of the wool (yarn) at one marked point with your thumb and then begin to wind the wool (yarn) evenly making sure it is neither too loose nor too tight. Work round and round the shade crossing over the top and bottom edge each time at the next marked point. Continue right round the shade, then secure the end of the wool (yarn).
To make the trimming, cut two $\frac{1}{2}$ inch wide strips of the basic lampshade covering material to the same length as the original piece for the shade. Wind wool (yarn) evenly and closely round and round this strip so that the material is completely covered. Turn the end under and stick round the edge of shade, overlapping about $\frac{1}{4}$ inch.

Materials

2 lampshade rings, one with lamp fitting (about 8 inches diameter)
Coloured lampshade covering (or iron thin fabric on to adhesive parchment)
1 oz. random shaded double-knitting wool (knitting worsted)
Clear all-purpose adhesive

Velvet-Striped Writing Case

It is surprisingly easy to create sophisticated effects by using interesting combinations of textures. Here an unbleached lining canvas has been striped with soft velvet in a glowing colour to make an elegant writing case. Choose the colour of the writing paper first, then key the cover fabrics to that. The measurements given are for a standard 8 inch by 6 inch pad but you can adjust them to fit any size.

Method

Measure the writing pad and add $\frac{1}{4}$ inch to each measurement. Cut two pieces of heavy cardboard to this size, and another strip the same depth, but only 1 inch wide for the spine.

Place these three pieces of cardboard side by side, the spine in the centre, touching each other, with the top and bottom edges absolutely level. Tape together as shown in diagram 1, where broken lines indicate edges of card under tape – inside of case.

Cut a piece of canvas 1 inch larger all round than the cardboard. Cover the outside of the case in three stages. Beginning by sticking the canvas *to one side only* (marked A in diagram 2), the cardboard should be exactly centred on the canvas. Mitre the corners by cutting away a triangle, (diagram 2), and slash at centre joins. Bring the surplus fabric round to the inside and stick down smoothly. Fold in the canvas at centre so that the fabric is stretched round the spine and stick the canvas to the spine. Then stick the canvas to the second main piece of cardboard. Mitre the corners, and bring the surplus fabric to the inside, as before.

Cut four strips of velvet ribbon, one of each

Materials

Writing pad (8 inch by 6 inch)
Matching envelopes
$\frac{1}{2}$ yard × 24 inch wide lining canvas
1 yard × $1\frac{1}{2}$ inch wide velvet ribbon
$\frac{5}{8}$ yard × 1 inch wide velvet ribbon
$\frac{3}{8}$ yard × $\frac{5}{8}$ inch wide velvet ribbon
1 yard × $\frac{3}{8}$ inch wide velvet ribbon
Heavy cardboard
Thin cardboard
Strong adhesive tape
Fabric adhesive

Velvet-striped writing case, coffee and cream coasters, straw-daisy plaque, matchboxes

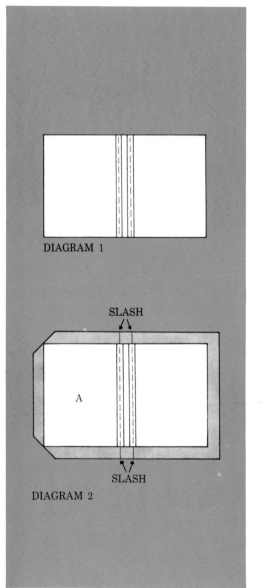

DIAGRAM 1

SLASH

A

SLASH

DIAGRAM 2

of the different widths, and each 2 inches deeper than the depth of the writing case. Stick these to the cover as illustrated, 1 inch apart and overlapping equally, top and bottom. Turn the ends over neatly and stick to the inside of the case. Stick a 1 inch wide length of velvet ribbon down the spine.

Cut two pieces of the narrowest ribbon, each 2 inches deeper than the depth of the case. Open up the case and fix the two pieces to the left-hand inside cover. Turn the ends under and stick very securely into position, leaving the ribbon loose enough to slip the envelopes underneath.

Cut a piece of canvas to the overall width measurement of the inside of the case plus 2 inches and to slightly less than the depth. Stick this neatly into place inside the case, under the ribbon loops.

Cut a piece of thin cardboard exactly the same size as the writing pad. Place this behind the pad. Cut a 6 inch length of the widest velvet ribbon, fold it diagonally round a corner of the pad to form a triangle, and stick the ends neatly to the back of the card behind the pad. Finish the remaining three corners in the same way and then stick the cardboard to the right hand inside cover very securely.

Coffee and Cream Coasters

There is nothing more cheering than a mug of steaming hot coffee – and nothing more distressing than a ring on a polished table-top. Pretty coaster mats made in contrasting shades of coffee and cream will protect your furniture.

Method

Cut a 4 inch diameter circle in linen or felt.
Bind the raw edge of the linen.
Stitch a circle of brown daisies round the edge of the linen mat, over the binding, or individual cream daisies in the centre of the felt mat, as illustrated.

Materials

Cream linen
Brown felt
Cream binding (for linen)
Brown and cream lace daisies or similar trimming

Matchbox Magic

Matchboxes assume a very elegant character when grouped in intriguing shapes and smartly covered. Use up odd scraps of pretty fabrics – or use vinyl for the kitchen – to make the most inexpensive, yet personal, presents. Half the fun is inventing different arrangements of the boxes.

Method

Group two, three or four boxes on a piece of stiff cardboard (diagram 1 shows the different positions of the boxes illustrated). When a pleasing arrangement has been achieved, draw round the outline of the grouped boxes making sure that they do not move. Cut out the shape with a sharp knife or scissors. Place the shape on another piece of cardboard, draw round it and cut out a second piece.

Using just a smear of adhesive, stick each piece of cardboard to the wrong side of the fabric and then cut out, leaving $\frac{1}{4}$ inch surplus fabric all round. Mitre the corners and clip into the angles (diagram 2). Fold the excess fabric over and glue it down to the cardboard.

Cut a $2\frac{1}{2}$ inch length of ribbon for each drawer. Fold the ribbon in half lengthways and glue cut ends inside the boxes so that a looped end protrudes as illustrated. Replace the matches in the boxes.

Glue the matchboxes into position on the wrong side of one piece of covered cardboard. Glue the second piece of covered cardboard on top and press down firmly. Leave the boxes under a weight until quite dry.

Materials

Boxes of matches
Fabric or self-adhesive vinyl to cover
Narrow ribbon
Stiff cardboard
Fabric adhesive

Matchbox magic

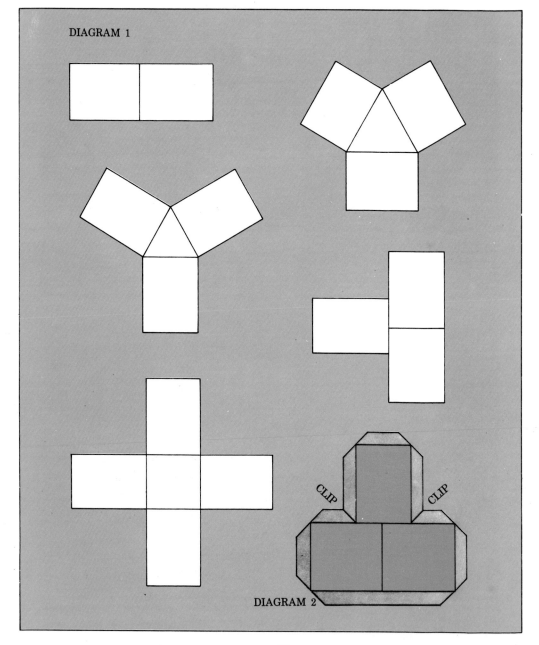

DIAGRAM 1

DIAGRAM 2

CLIP

CLIP

36

Kitchen

Tempt all your family to help you in the kitchen by making them gay aprons in tough denim or practical PVC.

Quick notes and shopping lists can be pinned on a decorative wall board, and rubber bands kept on a tidy wall dispenser. There is an attractive hanging rack for herbs and spices, and a useful heat-proof mat.

Pets have not been forgotten – wipe-clean mats will protect the floor around a dog's or cat's eating dish.

Hanging Spice Rack

A bamboo or woven straw table mat can be turned into a charming hanging rack for herbs and spices. Any thin wood will do for the inside as long as it can be cut with a sharp craft knife and joined with ½ inch steel pins – ⅛ inch balsa is particularly suitable.

Method

Cut pieces of wood as follows, and sandpaper smooth:

1 piece, 11 inches long by 2 inches wide – A
2 pieces, 11 inches long by 1½ inches wide – B
2 pieces, 2 inches square – C
2 pieces, 6 inches long by 1 inch wide – D
1 piece, 12 inches long by 1 inch wide – E
1 piece, 12 inches long by ¾ inch wide – F

Stick and pin the two ends C to the base A (diagram 1). Stick and pin the two sides B between (diagram 2).
Fold the mat in half and stick the two ends together. Stick this joined edge level with the front of the rack, overlapping equally at each end, then take the mat down over the front, under the base and up the back, sticking securely all the way – so that the folded edge extends about 2½ inches above the rack. Strengthen with pins through the mat into the wood at each side.

Materials

A bamboo or straw table mat 12 inches × 18 inches
Thin wood
Decorative transfer motifs
Self-adhesive labels
All-purpose adhesive
Tiny steel or panel pins

For the kitchen: rubber band dispenser, hanging spice rack, reminder board

SHOPPING LIST

1lb Tomatoes

2lb Pots

1 Large Cabbage

1 Doz Eggs (Large)

MIXED HERBS   SAGE   CAYENNE   THYME   PAPRIKA   ALLSPICE

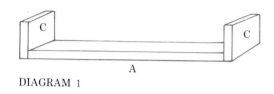

C   C

A

DIAGRAM 1

Stick the two 6 inch strips D behind the mat, positioning as illustrated, so that the lower edges are level with the base of the rack, and extending about 1½ inches above. Pin at the base to strengthen and drill a hole at the top of each, to hang.

Stick strip E along the top edge at the back of the mat, and strip F along the front. Decorate the back strip with transfer motifs, and stick herb and spice labels along the front.

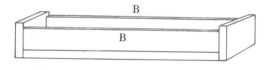

B

B

DIAGRAM 2

Kitchen Reminder Board

It is essential to be able to make a hasty
note or shopping list in the kitchen – and to
have somewhere to pin a reminder or a recipe.
This quick-to-assemble board combines both
functions.
All kinds of decoration are possible – sticky
seals, motifs cut from self-adhesive vinyl or
washable wallpaper or transfer would be
suitable.

Method

Make holes in the two top corners of the
hard table mat and thread cord through to
hang, knotting the ends securely at the back.
Cut the cork mat in half, and stick each piece
near the base, as illustrated. Stick the pad
securely above.
Cut a groove near the end of the pencil and
tie a length of cord round it. Fix the other
end through the top hole and secure it at the
back. Decorate the board with motifs to
match the kitchen scheme.

Materials

Hard table mat (about 9 inches by 10 inches)
Jotting pad (about 6 inches deep by 4 inches
    wide)
4 inch diameter circular cork mat
Pencil
Decorative motifs
Cord to hang
Clear all-purpose adhesive

Togetherness in the Kitchen

Really practical and straightforward aprons for the whole family: 'His' and 'Hers' are tough denim with a nautical air – 'It' has a smaller version in wipe-clean PVC (vinyl) (which can, of course, be lengthened as necessary). The halter neck adjusts to size automatically – just by pulling the ties.

If you do not want to rule squares, and have no graph paper, you can simply measure out the pattern, following the measurements indicated by the squares on the chart:

X shows you where to place the point of your compasses for the lower curve.

Method

Rule a sheet of paper into one-inch squares, use graph paper or measure (see above) out patterns for the aprons and pockets, following the diagram. Follow the lefthand straight line for the centre front fold of the aprons. Cut His apron in dark denim, with a pocket in the light shade, 9 inches deep by 14 inches wide. Cut Hers in light denim, with the pocket as shown on the pattern in the dark shade. Cut Its apron and the pocket in PVC (vinyl).

Bind each apron across the top (A–A), down the straight sides (below B) and round the lower edge, and all round the pocket except across the top, with narrow binding. Then bind the curved sides between A and B with wide binding, allowing the same amount as the narrow to show on the right side. Bind the top edge of the pocket in the same way. Pin the pocket in position and top-stitch securely into place, double-stitching firmly at the top corners.

Thread the cord through channels formed by wide binding at each side, looping it across the top and knotting cut ends to prevent fraying.

Materials

¾ yard each 36-inch wide light and dark denim (His and Hers)
An 18-inch square of PVC (vinyl) (Its)
½-inch wide bias binding
1-inch wide bias binding
2 yards piping or lacing cord (for each)

Aprons for all the family

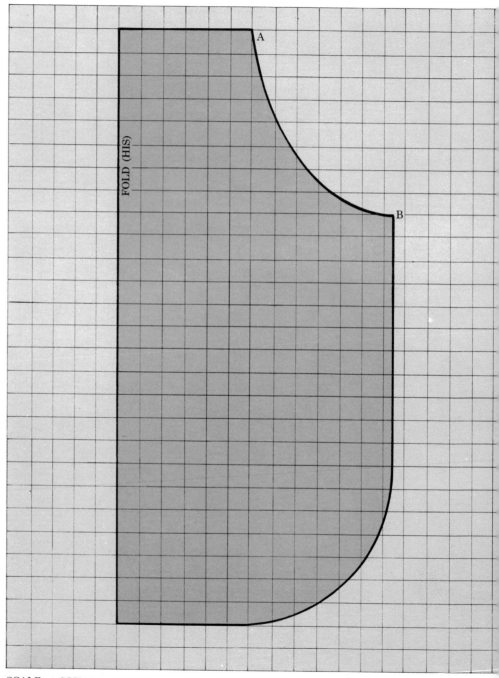

FOLD (HIS)

A

B

SCALE: 1 SQUARE=1 INCH

44

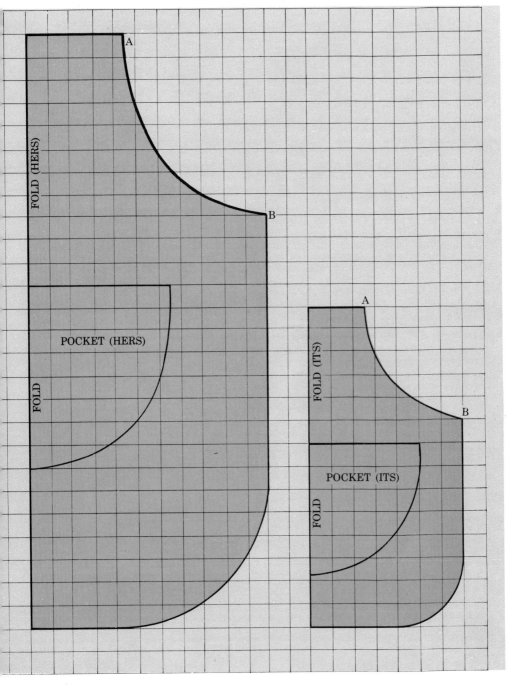

FOLD (HERS)

A

B

POCKET (HERS)

FOLD

FOLD (ITS)

A

B

POCKET (ITS)

FOLD

Rubber Band Dispenser

Use thin wood or ply – balsa is quick and easy to cut, using a sharp craft knife and a metal rule. Painted or decorated, this is a useful item to hang anywhere where a quick choice of the right-sized rubber band is needed.

Method

On a sheet of $\frac{1}{4}$ inch squared graph paper, draw out the shape following diagram 1. Rule five horizontal lines 1 inch apart as indicated. Cut this out to use as your pattern. Place the pattern on the wood and mark round the outline carefully. Cut out. Replace the paper pattern on the wood shape and mark the horizontal lines on the edges of the wood.
Cut out a notch ($\frac{3}{8}$ inch wide by $\frac{1}{4}$ inch deep) on the edge of a piece of paper, following the pattern in diagram 2. Placing the edge of the paper level with the edge of the wood, mark and cut a notch at each marked point.
Make a hole at the top of the wood shape, as indicated. Sandpaper all over until smooth. Paint, stain or varnish and decorate as desired. Make a loop of cord at the top to hang. Fit graduated elastic bands into the notches.

Materials

A piece of wood 6 inches deep by 3 inches wide by about $\frac{3}{8}$ inch thick
Cord to hang
Paint, stain or varnish
Decorative motifs
Assorted rubber bands
Sharp craft knife
Metal rule

Rubber band dispenser

DIAGRAM 1   SCALE: 1 SQUARE=$\frac{1}{4}$ INCH

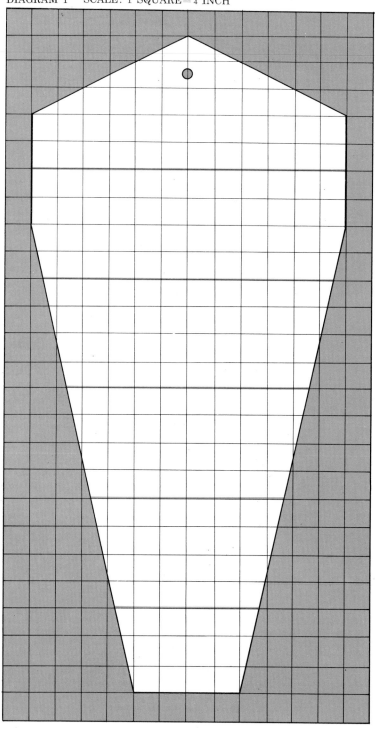

DIAGRAM 2 PATTERN FOR CUTTING NOTCH

Dog and Cat Dinner Mats

A place of his own for your dog, or cat, where he can eat his meals on an appropriately decorated wipe-clean mat – and you are left with a tidy floor!

Method

On a sheet of one inch squared paper, draw the dog or cat outline following the diagram (1 square = 1 inch). Cut the pattern out carefully, and place it on the paper back of the self-adhesive vinyl, reversing the way you want the animal to face. Draw round the pattern. Cut out the animal shape.
Cut the PVC (vinyl) to size and stick tape all round the edge to neaten. Cut along the centre of the tape with pinking shears to make a decorative edge.
Peel away the paper backing from the animal shape and stick into position in centre of the mat, smoothing it down from the middle to the edges.

Materials

Cloth-backed plain PVC (vinyl) approximately 15 inches by 18 inches.
Self-adhesive vinyl 11 inches by 14 inches.
Adhesive fabric tape ($\frac{1}{2}$ inch wide) to tone with vinyl.

Dog's dinner mat
Cat's dinner mat

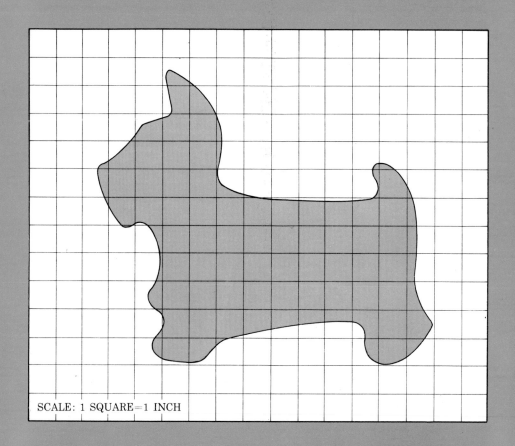

SCALE: 1 SQUARE=1 INCH

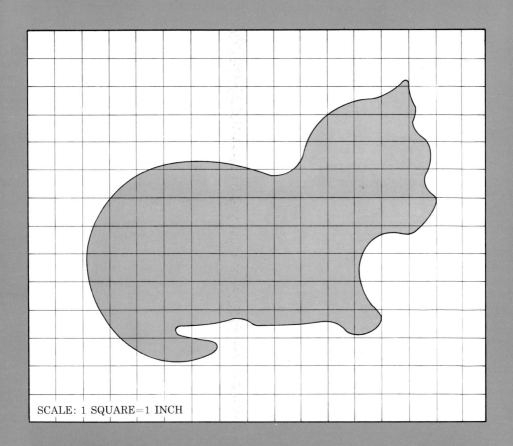

SCALE: 1 SQUARE=1 INCH

Teapot Stand

A heat-proof mat is one of those things you can't do without in the kitchen – and not just for teapots, either. But there is no reason why such a mundane and practical object should not look gay and individual, with motifs to match your decor.

A sheet of suitable sticky seals can be purchased, but motifs cut from self-adhesive vinyl create a similar effect. Alternatively cut designs from left-over scraps of kitchen wallpaper.

Materials

Heat-resistant mat (about 6 inches square)
Decorative motifs
Clear all-purpose adhesive (if the motifs are not self-adhesive)

Method

Cut out the motifs and move them around on your mat until you are satisfied with the arrangement.

Let the size of the motif and the shape of the mat dictate the arrangement (see diagram for examples). Peeling off backing or using adhesive, stick the motifs firmly into place.

Teapot stand and summer roses

Dining Room

Make some pretty paper roses for a year-round summery look.

For the dining table, you can make decorative mats. There are informal luncheon mats and braid place mats – match the braid to your colour scheme.

At breakfast, keep eggs warm in the amusing grandma and grandpa egg cosies.

Scandinavian Luncheon Mats

If you have never embroidered before, begin with cross-stitch. It is quick, easy, and gives a really professional result.

This versatile design, rather Scandinavian in feeling, can be adapted to articles of any size. It can be used in stripes for a cushion, as a border for a tablecloth – or for motifs to decorate a wide variety of home accessories. In these two examples, which show contrasting colour schemes, an even-weave linen-like dress fabric with about 20 threads to the inch has been used – and six strands of stranded embroidery cotton to give a bold effect. If you use a more finely woven fabric, use fewer strands – and remember your stitches will come up smaller. Each cross has been embroidered over two threads: to make your crosses larger on a finger fabric, embroider over three threads in each direction.

Method

Cut fabric to size, then begin by embroidering the double line of single stitches at the outer edge. Then count the number of crosses in this line and centre either a large or small motif, depending on the number of motifs which will fit into the complete line (see my two examples): embroider this the correct distance from the outer border, then complete the remaining motifs above and below. Follow with the decorative inner borders each side of the motifs, and finish with another row of single crosses. To balance the luncheon mats, work another double line at the opposite edge. And on the light, putty-coloured mat, the edge has been hem-stitched by hand, using three strands of the mid-brown used in the outer border.

Materials

Even-weave fabric
Stranded embroidery thread in five different shades

Scandinavian luncheon mats

58

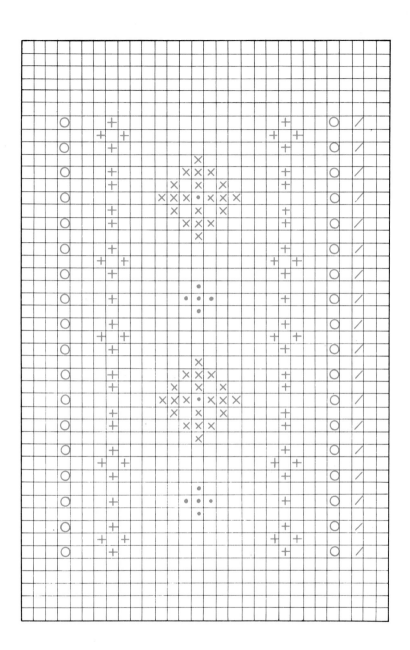

KEY

LIGHT BACKGROUND	DARK BACKGROUND
/ DARK BROWN	/ DARK BROWN
○ MID BROWN	○ LIGHT CORN
+ BRIGHT LEAF GREEN	+ LIME GREEN
× LIME GREEN	× LIGHT BLUE
• OLIVE GREEN	• LIGHT OLIVE GREEN

Summer Roses

A bunch of paper roses in sunshine colours to brighten the dullest winter's day. Shade them from red through orange and yellow or simply make them in a single colour – it is just as effective.

Method

To make one rose
Trace the petal shape and cut it out in thin cardboard to use as a pattern. With the grain of the paper running vertically, (see arrows) cut five petals out of two layers of crepe paper, deep red on top, orange behind. Place the dull surfaces of the paper facing so that the shiny side is outside. Cut out five more pairs of petals, this time just a little larger than the cardboard pattern and with orange on top and yellow behind.
Using solid stick adhesive, stick each pair of petals together at the tip, sides and base. Now 'cup' the lower half of each petal as follows: holding the petal, place your thumbs in the middle and gently stretch the crepe paper so that it forms a cupped, petal shape. Turn the petal over and cup the upper half from the back, so that the tip of the petal curls over backwards.
Cut a length of florist's wire and hook the end. Wrap a scrap of cotton wool over the hook and mould it into a ball about the size of a pea. Cut a 2 inch diameter circle of yellow crepe paper (or use green) and place it centrally over the cotton wool ball. Bring the crepe edges down and secure tightly close under the cotton wool with fine wire or thread.
Now take a red and orange petal and roll it lengthways round the yellow tip of the wire, quite tightly. Stick the base of the petal

Materials

Crepe paper in deep leaf green, red, orange and yellow.
Florists' wire
Thin garden canes, 18 inches long
Cotton wool
Fine wire or thread
Adhesive tape
Solid adhesive in stick form
Fabric adhesive

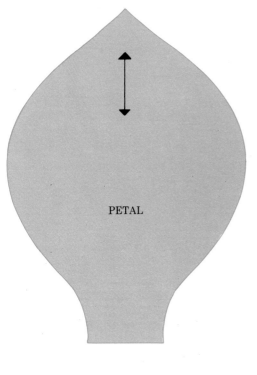

PETAL

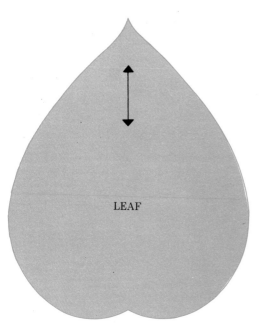

LEAF

round the wire close under the tip. Follow with another red and orange petal, exactly opposite the first and then stick the three remaining red and orange petals round the stalk, each new petal half overlapping the previous one and the lower edges always level. Continue in the same way with the five orange and yellow petals. Wire the base to hold the petals securely then re-cup and curl where necessary before pushing the petals together with your hands.

Fix a garden cane to the wire with adhesive tape for the stem.

Trace off the leaf shape and make a cardboard pattern.

Cut out two shapes in doubled green crepe paper (grain as arrows). Stick each doubled leaf together as for the petals, inserting a 6 inch length of wire straight down the centre of each. The rest of the wire extends from the bottom of the leaf for a stem.

Cut a strip of green crepe paper, 18 inches long and $\frac{1}{2}$ inch wide, the grain running across. Stick one end of the strip round the base of the petals, wind it round several times to secure and then gradually twist it round and down the stem, binding in first one leaf and then the second. Secure the end of the strip with adhesive tape. Cup and curl the leaves slightly in the same way as for the petals.

Braid and ribbon mats

Braid and Ribbon Mats

Attractive place mats give distinction to the simplest meal and whether it is 'just the family' or a formal dinner party, it is important to set your table with style. By making sets of place mats in a linen-like woven fabric and decorating them with braids and ribbons, you can ring the changes with your table settings as often as you like. A set of six mats can be made from $\frac{1}{2}$ yard of 36 inch wide fabric.

Method

Cut the fabric to size, following the thread. Draw three or four threads about $\frac{5}{8}$ inch from the edge, all the way round. Zig-zag the inner edge on the sewing machine – or hem-stitch, by hand – and then pull away the remaining outer parts to form a fringe.
Cut the ribbon or braid into strips to fit the mat, allowing $\frac{1}{2}$ inch at each end to turn under. Pin or tack into position, making sure it is absolutely flat, then hem-stitch neatly all the way round.
The braids used for the mats illustrated are 2 inches wide (the single stripe), $1\frac{1}{2}$ inches (silk embroidery on black ribbon), $1\frac{1}{4}$ inches (two-colour woven) and 1 inch (the daisies).

Materials

For each mat
A piece of woven fabric, 9 inches by 12 inches
$\frac{1}{4}$ yard of braid or ribbon for *each* stripe

Grandma and Grandpa Egg Cosies

Whether you are seven or seventy, it is cheering to find Grandma and Grandpa thoughtfully keeping your eggs warm when you're late for breakfast!

Method

Rule a sheet of paper into half-inch squares or use dressmaker's squared graph paper which shows half-inch markings. Draw the cosy pattern following the diagram.
Cut the shape twice in flesh felt for each cosy: cut a 1¼ inch diameter circle for Grandpa's nose.
Oversew the two cosy pieces all round the curved edge, leaving lower edges open. Turn to right side.

To make *Grandma*, stitch embroidered ribbon round the base of the cosy, join the ribbon at centre back. Stitch lace level with the top edge of the ribbon.
Cut a piece of cardboard 6 inches deep and wind double-knitting wool (knitting worsted) round it fifteen times for the hair. Tie the loops temporarily on both sides, slide off the cardboard and tie loosely at the centre. Stitch centre to centre top of cosy, towards the front. Then bring the loops down, catch securely over side seam and remove ties. Wind wool (yarn) round the cardboard again fifteen times, and tie as before. Stitch centre behind centre of first piece, then catch loops across back of head, removing ties as before. Wind wool (yarn) ten times round a 4 inch deep piece of cardboard: slide off, tie a knot, and stitch securely to top of head.
Embroider mouth as indicated on the pattern in stem stitch.

Materials

A piece of flesh-coloured felt 9 inches by 6½ inches
A scrap of black felt
Grey double-knitting wool (knitting worsted) (Grandma)
Beige textured knitting yarn (Grandpa)
6 inches of embroidered ribbon (Grandma)
6 inches of ⅜ inch wide guipure lace (Grandma)
9 inches of 1 inch wide white ribbon (Grandpa)
2½ inches of 1½ inch wide tartan ribbon (Grandpa)
2 × ⅝ inch diameter brass curtain rings (Grandma)
1 × 1 inch diameter brass curtain ring (Grandpa)
Tiny gilt beads, fine chain or gold cord (Grandpa)
Pearls or beads (Grandma)
Red stranded embroidery thread (Grandma)
Fabric adhesive

Position curtain rings for eye glasses and sew into place at the centre and at each side. Trace eye pattern and cut out in black felt: stick in the centre of each ring.
Stitch beads over seam at each side, just below hair, for ear-rings.

To make *Grandpa,* stitch white ribbon round the lower edge of the cosy, folding the ribbon back 1¼ inches at each side of the centre front, so that the cut ends are level with the seams. For the neck bow, fold 2 inches of ribbon into three widthways; gather the centre and pull it up tight. Then fold a ¼ inch strip into three, wrap round gathered centre, trim ends and join at back. Stitch securely over centre front of collar.
Gather nose circle all round outer edge: put a scrap of cotton wool in the centre and draw up tightly. Stitch to face (from behind) at X. Cut a piece of cardboard 3 inches deep; wind textured yarn round it about twenty times (according to thickness) for the moustache. Slide off carefully and tie at the centre. Stitch securely just below the nose.
Cut a piece of cardboard 1 inch deep by 4 inches long, and wind yarn round it about 100 times for the hair. Thread a needle with matching thread and catch end securely over the side seam, 2¾ inches above the lower edge. Place the cardboard across the back of the head, distributing the yarn evenly over 3 inches and catch the loops along the top edge of the card securely across the back of the head. Slide cardboard out gently, then catch a few lower loops at the front of the face at each side, and the remainder lightly across the back of the head.

Stitch a curtain ring into position for a monocle, with a chain or string of tiny beads to hold it to the side seam. Trace the eye pattern off and cut two in black felt. Stick them to the face, centring one inside the monocle.

Grandma and grandpa egg cosies

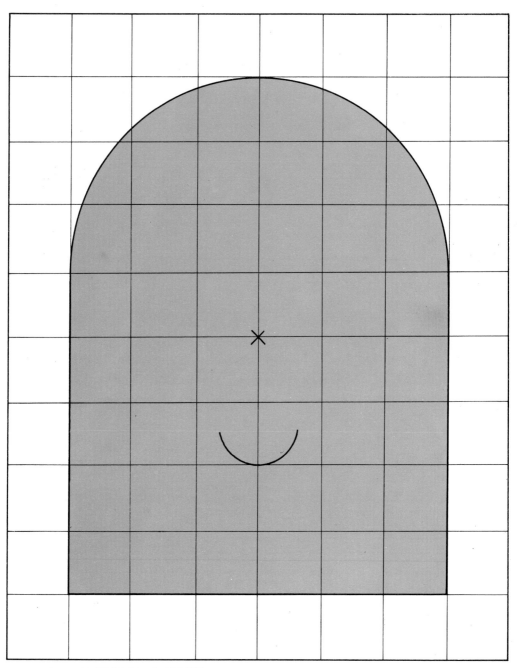

SCALE: 1 SQUARE=$\frac{1}{2}$ INCH

EYE

Bedroom

You can make the bedroom look very pretty with this selection of makes. Pamper yourself with a patterned breakfast set and tray cloth.

To decorate a bedroom chair, make the rosebud gingham cushion; for the dressing table, there is a frilly lace lampshade and a matching set of wastepaper basket, tissue-box cover and picture frame. Add charm to the walls with an elegant Edwardian silhouette.

Rosebud Gingham Cushion

Cushions are one of the most delightful ways to dress a room – and you can reflect your own personality and taste in the way you use trimmings. The instructions here are for a basic cushion but they can be easily adapted to make cushions of different shapes and sizes. Use the different design ideas in this book for trims and decoration; Scandinavian cross-stich embroidery, for example; the nursery wall hangings; stripes of woven or embroidered braids. You can also try interesting textural effects such as velvet ribbons on canvas, as used for the writing case.

Materials

2 × 14 inch squares of check gingham
1½ yards of 1 inch deep cotton fringe
Embroidered rosebud motifs
2 × 14 inch squares of fine cotton for the inner cushion
Filling

Method

Cut the fabric to size and stitch the fringe to the right side of one piece ½ inch in from the edge, with the outer edge of the fringe towards the centre of the cushion. Stitch the trimming into position on the front of the cushion. With right sides facing,
join the front and back of the cushion on three sides following the stitching line of the fringe. Trim seams, clip corners and turn to right side.
Make up the inner cushion in the same way, omitting fringe and decoration. Stuff firmly, then turn in raw edges and slip-stitch together. Fit inner cushion inside cover, turn in edges of remaining side, and slip-stitch neatly. Alternatively, insert a zip or touch-and-close fastening, so that the cover can be removed more easily.

For the bedroom: rosebud gingham cushion, embroidery and lace lampshade, Edwardian silhouette

Embroidery and Lace Lampshade

Perfect for a dressing table, this frilly lace shade looks delicately fragile. Yet it is the simplest thing to whisk off the cover, wash it out and slip it back into place when dry.

The directions and quantities given are for 3 inch wide lace, but you can, of course, use a narrower lace, in which case you will require a longer length – or a wider lace, when you will need less. To adapt the instructions to the lace of your choice, just divide the width of your lace into twenty-four to calculate the number of strips (about $6\frac{1}{2}$–7 inches long) you will need.

And if you cannot find a lace that combines embroidery, use separate strips embroidered flowers or ribbon. Although the directions are for a 6 inch deep, 7 inch diameter shade, the design can be used for any cylindrical lampshade of different proportions.

Method

Measure round the outer edge of a ring and add 1 inch. Cut a strip of parchment this length by 6 inches deep.

Using double thread, oversew one long edge of the parchment round one ring: do not finish stitching overlap. Oversew the other edge round the second ring. Trim overlap, if necessary, and stick with double-sided tape or adhesive. Finish stitching at top and bottom of join.

To make the cover, cut a piece of net 8 inches deep by 25 inches long. Cut the $1\frac{1}{2}$ yards of lace into eight equal $6\frac{3}{4}$ inch lengths.

Leaving $\frac{1}{2}$ inch of net clear along top, bottom and both side edges, stitch the strips of lace side-by-side to cover the net (see diagram). Right sides facing, join the two short side edges of the net. Turn and stitch a $\frac{1}{4}$ inch hem

Materials

2×7 inch diameter lampshade rings, one with lamp fitting
$1\frac{1}{2}$ yards of 3 inch wide embroidered frilled nylon lace
White nylon net
White lampshade parchment
Narrow round elastic
Double-sided tape (or all-purpose adhesive)

72

all round the top and bottom edges.
Turn to the right side. Thread narrow elastic
through the top and bottom channels and fit
the cover over the shade with upper and
lower edgings overlapping equally. Draw up
the elastic so that the cover fits the shade.

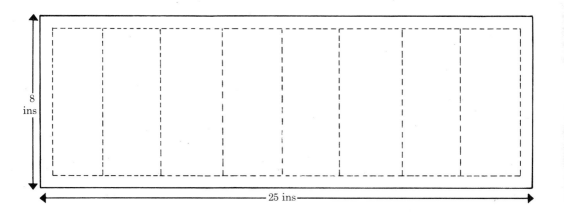

8 ins

25 ins

Flowered Breakfast Set

Certain to cheer the dullest morning, this gay breakfast set is not just pretty – it is practical too.

Method

Draw the pattern for the *tea cosy* as follows. Draw a 9 inch diameter circle and mark the centre, point A. Rule a straight line from the top edge of the circle to the bottom, through A (see diagram 1). Mark point B 2½ inches below A, and draw line C–D at right-angles to A–B. Mark point E ¾ inch from the edge of the circle (point F), and draw line G–H parallel to C–D. Now extend line E–F ¼ inch to point J (1 inch above point E), and draw line K–L, 6 inches long, centre J and parallel to G–H. Then join K–G and L–H. Finally, with the point of your compasses at A, draw an arc between points K and L. Cut out, omitting the shaded section at the base, so that it looked like diagram 2.

Draw a 5 inch diameter circle for the base. Allowing ½ inch turnings all round, cut out the cosy pattern four times and the base circle twice from the printed cotton. If you are using the design of the fabric for special effect, it is a good idea to cut out all three items in the set first, cutting the linings of the cosies and the base pieces from the remaining fabric.

Cut the cosy pattern twice more, and the base circle once, in doubled wadding. This time cut same size as the pattern, without allowing turnings.

Materials

¼ yard of 48 inch wide printed cotton
Washable wadding
½ yard of ¾ inch wide double-edged broderie anglaise
½ yard of ¾ inch wide frilled broderie anglaise
1½ yards narrow broderie anglaise or guipure lace
½ yard of ½ inch wide white tape or binding
Narrow round elastic

Flowered breakfast set and tray cloth

74

To make up the tea cosy

Tack a layer of double wadding to the wrong side of each lining piece for the cosy and to the base circle lining. Mark the edge of the pattern shape on the wrong side of the two outer cosy pieces, then place each piece onto the linings, with right sides facing. Stitch all round, leaving the straight lower edges open. Trim seams, clip curves and corners and turn both to the right side. Turn in the raw edges and tack.

Pad and stitch the base pieces in the same way remembering to leave a section unstitched to turn to right side. Use slip-stitch to close the section. Oversew to join the straight lower edges of each half of the cosy to the base, with corners meeting. Stitch the tape or binding to the wrong side of the double-edged broderie anglaise, forming a channel. Join the short ends to make a circle. Thread elastic through and draw up the circle so that it holds the top of the cosy together, as illustrated.

To make the egg cosy

Rule a sheet of paper into half-inch squares (or use graph paper), as diagram 3. Draw line A–B (4 inches long), then A–C and B–D (each $1\frac{3}{4}$ inches). Mark point E (4 inches above A–B) and, with the point of your compasses at F, draw an arc to join E–D, and with the point at G, join E–C.

Allowing $\frac{1}{2}$ inch turnings all round, cut out the pattern in cotton four times. Cut the pattern out twice more in single wadding without turnings.

Tack the single layer of wadding to the wrong side of each lining piece. With right sides facing, join all round the top edge, leaving the lower edge open. Trim and clip seam.

Mark the edge of the pattern shape on the right side of one outer cosy piece, stitch frilled broderie anglaise along this line, with the scalloped edge of the broderie anglaise towards the centre (diagram 4). Allow a little extra at the top of the cosy. Place the second outer cosy piece on top of this trimmed piece, right sides facing and, following the previous stitching line, stitch all round, but leaving lower edge open. Trim and slip seam and turn the cosy to right side. Fit the padded lining inside the cosy outer. Turn in the edges neatly and slip-stitch to close.

To make the *napkin*

Cut a 12 inch square of printed cotton. Neaten the edges with zig-zag stitch, or by turning a narrow hem. Trim with narrow broderie anglaise.

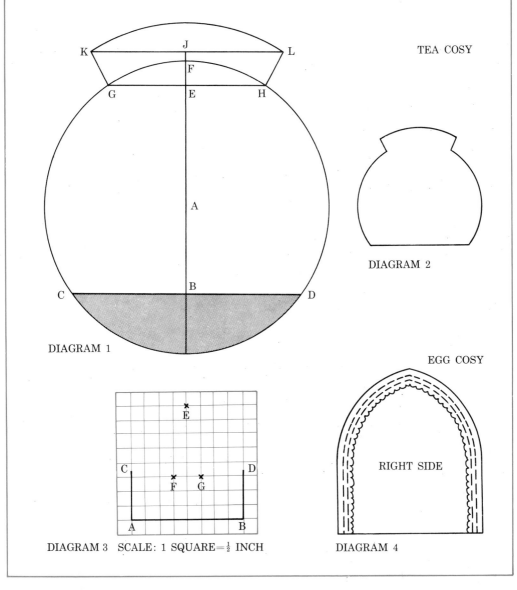

TEA COSY

DIAGRAM 1

DIAGRAM 2

DIAGRAM 3   SCALE: 1 SQUARE=$\frac{1}{2}$ INCH

EGG COSY

RIGHT SIDE

DIAGRAM 4

77

Edwardian Silhouettes

This artistic looking collage is easier to do than it looks at first sight. The colour scheme and decoration can be based on the figure shown here or the basic outline can be trimmed in different ways.

Method

Cut the cardboard and background paper to size. Stick the green paper on the mount leaving a 1½ inch border all round.
Trace the outline of the silhouette and cut out the shape very carefully. Place the paper pattern flat onto the black paper and draw round the outline with a white pencil. Cut out very carefully. Stick the figure and the parasol in the centre of the background and draw in the parasol handle and ferrule using a felt pen. Cut scraps of lace for the collar, cuffs, hem and parasol. Trim and stick into position. Stick ribbons and flowers in an attractive arrangement. Stick gilt braid all round the edge of the mount for a frame. Fix the picture hanger to the back.

Materials

Stiff dark grey-green cardboard, 13 inches by 10 inches for mount
Lime green cartridge (construction) paper, 10 inches by 7 inches for background
Thin black cartridge (construction) paper
Artificial flowers in assorted colours
Narrow white lace edging
Scraps of ribbon
1½ yards gilt braid
Fabric adhesive
Self-adhesive picture hanger

Edwardian silhouette collage

Breakfast Tray Cloth

If you can darn, you can make this pretty
tray cloth – and it is much more fun than
mending socks. Choose a yarn to match the
colours of the flowered breakfast set. An
even-weave embroidery linen may be used,
but an evenly woven dress fabric, with the
large selection of colours available, is a less
expensive alternative.

Method

Cut your fabric to size, following the thread.
Draw three or four threads about $\frac{3}{4}$ inch
from the edge, all the way round. Zig-zag the
inner edge on the sewing machine – or hem-
stitch, by hand. Pull away the remaining
outer threads to form a fringe. Now draw a
single thread about $\frac{3}{8}$ inch from the inner
edge of the fringe, *along one side only*. Thread
your needle with three strands of
contrasting knitting yarn. Bring the needle
up from the wrong side, $\frac{3}{8}$ inch from one end
of the drawn thread line and 'darn' along it,
weaving over six threads and under one –
until you reach the other end. Stop $\frac{3}{8}$ inch
from the end and draw a thread at right-
angles to continue down the next side in the
same way. Repeat until all four sides are
'darned'.
Now draw a thread, in the same way, eleven
threads in from this first border and weave a
similar border inside the first one. Then
weave a third border, five threads in from the
second one.
Finally, working on the outer, first, border
only, weave in and out all the way round,
see diagram. Take the wool backwards and
forwards under each existing stitch, forming
a wavy line held in place by the first row of
straight stitches.

Materials

A piece of even-weave fabric, about 26 threads
   to the inch, 18 inches by 24 inches (or to
   fit your tray)
4-ply random-shaded knitting yarn (or use
   strands from 3 different coloured yarns)
A medium tapestry needle

Photograph on page 75

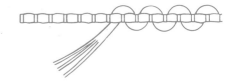

Dressing Table Set

Dress up your bedroom with this sophisticated set in a softly toning velvet. The 'velvet' is a quick cheat – self adhesive velour – the lazy way to a luxury finish. Amounts for the braids and trims vary according to the size of the articles. The quantities given were used for the articles illustrated.

Method

Measure round the outside of the bin and add 1 inch to the measurement. Cut a strip of velour to this measurement by the depth of the bin. Peel off the paper backing and stick the velour round the bin smoothly. Stick the fringe round the top edge as shown.

For the tissue box cover:
Measure the length and width of the box top and add $\frac{1}{4}$ inch to each measurement. Measure each of the sides in the same way, adding $\frac{1}{4}$ inch to each measurement. Cut pieces of cardboard for the top and the four sides to these dimensions.
Remove the perforated opening from the top of the box and measure its position. Place it on the cardboard cut for the top and draw round it. Cut out the shape with a sharp pointed knife.
Fix the sides and ends of the box top using adhesive tape and secure the four corners in the same way.
Cut pieces of velour to the same measurements as the cardboard pieces. Do not attempt to cut a hole in the velour for the box top. Simply stick the velour in position and then cut out the hole with a sharp knife, working from inside.
Stick narrow trimming round the edge of the

Materials

1 yard of 18 inch wide self-adhesive velour paper
Cylindrical metal waste-paper bin (about 7 inches diameter and $8\frac{1}{4}$ inches high)
Box of paper tissues
Heavy cardboard
$\frac{3}{4}$ yard fringe (and braid if fringe is plain), for bin
$\frac{1}{2}$ yard narrow embroidered trim, for box
$1\frac{1}{4}$ yards wider matching braid
$\frac{1}{4}$ yard gilt braid, for frame
$\frac{1}{4}$ yard narrow embroidered trim
Adhesive tape
Fabric adhesive

Dressing table set

top opening and then stick wider braid over
joins, round the top and down the sides.

For the frame:
Cut two circles of cardboard $4\frac{1}{2}$ inches in
diameter and then cut a smaller circle in the
centre of one, $2\frac{1}{2}$ inches in diameter. Cut a
piece of velour into a circle $4\frac{1}{2}$ inches in
diameter, and stick it to the frame. On the
wrong side, cut out the smaller circle in the
velour. Stick embroidered trimming round
the edge of the smaller circle.
Fit a photograph behind the frame and hold
it in position with tape. Stick the back of the
frame to the front round the outer edge.
Trim with gilt braid. Make a strut by
cutting a piece of cardboard 4 inches deep by
$1\frac{1}{4}$ inches wide. Score one end $\frac{5}{8}$ inch from the
end. Stick the strut into position on the back
of the frame.

Nursery and Playroom

Here are several bright colourful items to make for the children's room. There are two collages – one

showing the Owl and the Pussycat and one called Toadstool Cottage. Young children will love the pixie ring mobile.

On a more practical note, which mothers will appreciate, there is a cuddly rabbit pyjama case and gay tidy bags – one for a boy and one for a girl.

The Owl and The Pussycat

This colourful wall hanging in collage uses a woven table mat for the background. Here is the romantic owl with his pussycat friend sailing away in their beautiful pea-green boat and not forgetting to take some honey and plenty of money!

Method

Make a ¾ inch hem along the two long edges of the mat. If fabric is being used, bind all four edges first. Using 1 inch to 1 square graph or dressmaker's squared paper, copy the squared diagram. Trace off the separate pieces to use as patterns to be cut out in felt as follows.

Trace the outline of the owl, following the broken lines at his base and cut out the shape in brown felt. Cut the wings in dark brown felt and stick them at each side of the body. Trace the chest and forehead in three sections, following the broken lines to join them. Cut the largest shape in deep beige, the middle one in light beige and the smallest shape in stone colour. Stick the three shapes into position on the owl's body, one on top of the other.

Cut two 1¼ inch diameter circles in bright yellow felt for the eyes and stitch yellow guipure lace round the edges. Stick a large white lace daisy and a small black one in the centre of each eye. Stick the eyes into place with the orange beak between.

Trace the cat's body, following the broken lines at the top and the bottom and cut out in pale grey felt. Cut the head separately in the same colour. Trace off the cat's white front, following the upper broken line. Edge the front with white lace and stick down on to the body.

Materials

A woven table mat or a piece of blue fabric about 18 inches by 12 inches.
Matching binding if fabric is used
2 thin garden canes about 20 inches long
¾ yard of narrow card
Coloured felt
Braid, beads, buttons, sequins, flowers and lace to trim
Stranded embroidery thread, black
Fabric adhesive

For the nursery: collages and mobile

Trace the features off onto thin paper and
tack the paper in position on the head.
Embroider the mouth through the paper and
mark the position of the nose and eyes with
tacking stitches. Tear the paper away gently.
Narrow black braid, cut in half, can be used
for the eyes or embroider them in stem
stitch. If you decide to use embroidery, work
before removing the paper.
Stick the head to the top of the body. Catch
beads at each side to hang as illustrated.
Cut out the boat in bright green felt. Stick
the boat into position over the bases of the
owl and the pussycat, following the diagram
and your pattern. Trace and cut out the honey
jar and the money, embroidering the latter
and tying a scrap of wool round the top.
Stick these two pieces inside the boat.
Embroider the cat's whiskers and stick
flowers behind her ear. The boat can be
trimmed with a band of braid and wide and
narrow braid can be used for the waves of
the sea.
The crescent moon is cut in yellow felt and
the sequin stars are stitched into place with
a tiny glass bead in the centre.
Finally, thread the canes through the
channels at top and bottom and fix the cord
at the top to hang the wall hanging.

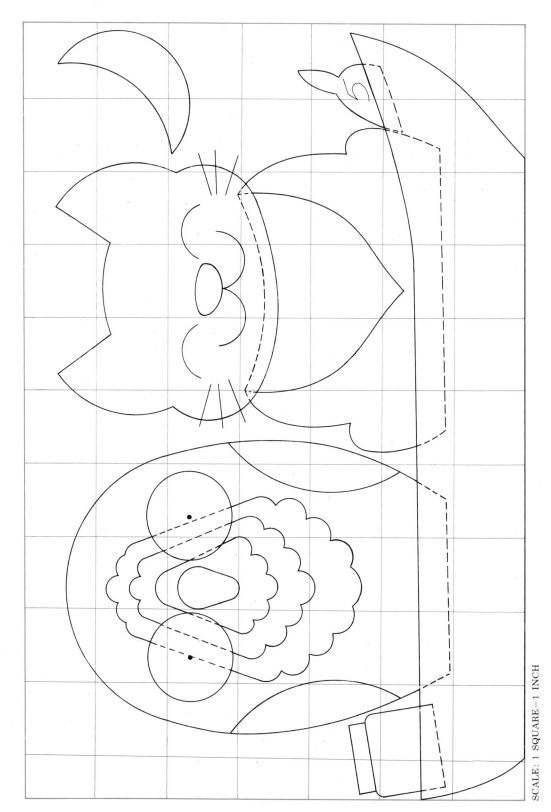

SCALE: 1 SQUARE=1 INCH

Pixie Ring Mobile

Five little pixies jigging merrily around make a perfect mobile for the nursery.

Method

Trace off and cut out separate paper patterns for one hand, the jerkin and the trousers, following the broken lines for the hand and trousers. Cut a 3 inch diameter half-circle for the hat.

Cut the hand shape out twice in flesh coloured felt and the jerkin and trousers twice each in gay coloured felt. Cut out the hat shape once in a felt to match either the jerkin or the trousers.

Stitch two small coloured beads down the centre of one jerkin piece for front buttons. Place the back jerkin piece flat and stick a hand at each end of the sleeve as shown in the diagram. Stick one trouser piece to the jerkin back putting adhesive on the upper part only and positioning as shown.

Cut a piece of pipe cleaner 4 inches long and bend it into the shape of the coloured line in the diagram. Stick it into position.

Stick the second trouser piece over the first and finally the front of the jerkin. Spread adhesive all over sleeves and across top and down each side.

To make the head, pierce a small hole in a table tennis ball with a long needle and then paint the ball flesh-coloured. When the paint is dry, push the ball down over the protruding pipe cleaner.

To make the hair, cut a piece of cardboard about 4 inches deep and wind the brown wool (yarn) round it about 15 times. Slide the loops off the cardboard and tie tightly in the middle. Cut the ends and spread out the wool (yarn) into a circle. Stick the wool (yarn) to

Materials

5 table tennis balls
Felt squares in bright colours
Flesh-coloured poster paint
Flesh-coloured felt
Black poster paint, ink or small adhesive labels
Pipe cleaners
Brown double knitting wool (knitting worsted), about 4 yards
Large and small coloured beads
9 inch diameter lampshade ring
1 small brass curtain ring
$\frac{7}{8}$ yard braid trimming
Black sewing thread
Black button thread
Fabric adhesive
Clear all-purpose adhesive
Tracing paper

Detail of pixie in pixie ring mobile

90

the ball, the tied centre at the crown and trim
the ends neatly. Paint in the eyes. Form the
hat into a cone and stick the straight edges
together. Smear a little adhesive round the
brim of the hat and stick the hat onto the
hair. Make four more pixies in the same way.
To make up the mobile, knot the end of a
piece of black sewing thread and catch it
firmly to the top of a hat. Slide a large bead
to rest on top of the hat and then tie the
other end of the thread to the lampshade
ring, about 6 inches above the figure.
Fix the remaining pixies equally around the
circle in the same way.
Cut four 15 inch lengths of black button
thread. Loop each one through the curtain
ring and knot about 1½ inches above the cut
ends of each pair. Then tie each doubled
thread at quarterly intervals round the ring.
Glue braid round the ring to neaten.

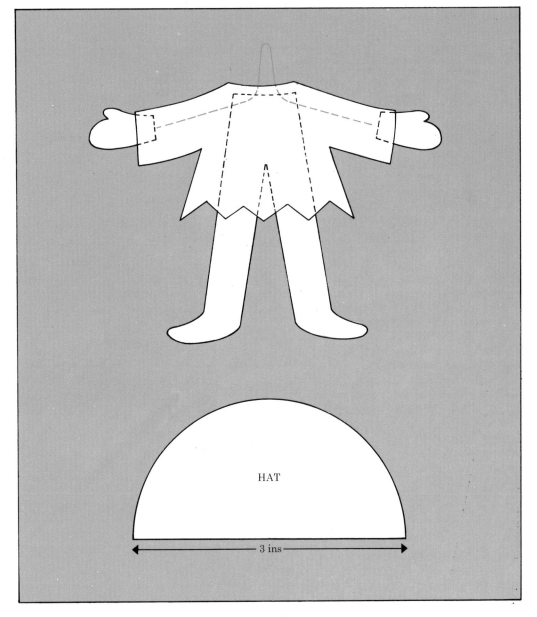

HAT

3 ins

Bunny Pyjama Case

A small child's pyjamas will tuck away tidily inside this friendly little bunny.

He is simple to make, too – all squares and circles! Make him in a soft, fleecy fabric with a slight stretch to give him a cuddly, rounded shape.

Method

On a sheet of squared graph or dressmaker's paper, (1 square = 1 inch), draw a pattern following the diagram. Use compasses to draw all the curves – the small x shows where to place the point of the compasses in each case.

Cut the body piece out once, the head, ear, upper foot and sole twice each, and the paw four times, all in cotton jersey, fleece side up. Cut out the ear twice more in pink fabric. Then cut the ear twice more in buckram, a little smaller all round than the pattern, tapering the sides slightly so that it is only about 1 inch wide across the base. Cut out the sole twice more in stiff cardboard, and a little smaller than the pattern.

Right sides facing, fold the body piece as indicated by the vertical broken line between notches on the pattern, so that the edges overlap for the centre back opening. Tack at the top and join the seam below the point x. With the right side of the fabric inside, join the lower edge, and run gathering threads round the front and back edge at the top.

With right sides facing, join the two head pieces, leaving the lower edge open between notches. Join to front and back of body, drawing up the gathers to fit, and distributing them evenly round the neck. Turn the *head only* to the right side, and

Materials

¼ yard of 48 inch wide fleece-surfaced cotton jersey
Pink felt about 5 inches by 7 inches for the inner ears
Checked gingham 10 inches × 12 inches
½ yard of ¼ inch wide ribbon for trouser straps
Scraps of pink and black felt for features
White wool (yarn)
Stiff cardboard
Buckram
Filling
Narrow round hat elastic
Fabric adhesive (optional)

Bunny pyjama case

94

stuff. Then oversew the lower edges securely together. Turn body to right side.

Gather the curved edge of the upper foot. With right sides facing, pin round the curved edge of the sole, distributing gathers evenly, then draw up to fit and stitch. Stick cardboard stiffening to the wrong side of the sole, turn in raw edges and slip-stitch together. Stitch straight edge securely to lower edge of body front, over-lapping slightly at one side. Repeat with second foot.

With right sides facing, join two paw pieces all round the curved edge. Turn to right side and stuff. Turn in raw edges and slip-stitch together, gathering slightly. Stitch to the body along side fold, positioning 1 inch below head. Repeat with second paw.

With right sides facing, join a fleece ear and a pink ear piece, leaving the lower edge open. Clip seam and turn to right side. Slip buckram inside, turn raw edges inside and slip-stitch together. Catch the two corners of the ear together and stitch each ear securely to the top of the head.

For the rabbit's hair, wind double-knitting wool (knitting worsted) about thirty times round a 2½ inch deep piece of cardboard. Tie the loops tightly on one edge, slide off and stitch to the top of the head between the ears. Trace off the nose and eye pattern and cut out in felt. Stick or appliqué them to the face. To make the rabbit's baggy trousers, cut two pieces of gingham 5 inches deep by 12 inches wide. Join the short sides, turn the top edge under and stitch, to form a narrow channel. Join the back and front for 1 inch only in the middle of the lower edge. Turn under a narrow hem for each trouser leg and gather. Fit on the rabbit and draw each up round the back of each foot. Thread elastic through the top channel and draw up to fit round the body. Stitch ribbon at each side for shoulder straps, catching to the top of the body close to head.

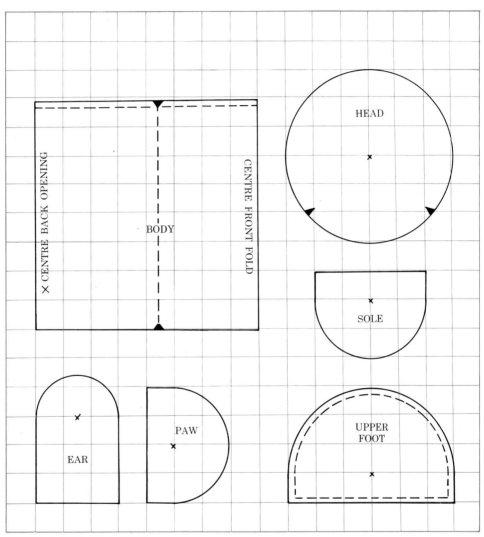

SCALE: 1 SQUARE=1 INCH

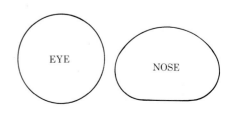

Toadstool Cottage

This charming wall-hanging for the nursery has been worked on a rather coarsely woven table mat but any fabric with a distinctive weave would be as effective. Add to the basic pattern from your own collection of pretty scraps.

Method

Turn a hem about 1 inch deep on both short edges. If using fabric, bind all four edges first. Copy the toadstool design onto squared paper, (1 square equals 1 inch). Trace off the separate outlines as follows and cut out the patterns in felt.
Following the broken lines at the top, trace the mushroom stalk and cut out in cream felt. Trace the door following the broken lines at the bottom and cut out in brown. Short pieces of black braid can be stuck on for door hinges and a small curtain ring stitched on for a door knocker. A wooden bead has been used for the handle. Stick the completed door onto the stalk with the grey door step over the lower door.
The small window is cut in pale blue felt and edged with a narrow strip of black braid cut lengthways.
The lattice is simply criss-crossed lines of embroidery cotton. The bell-pull is made from small gilt beads threaded onto thread and left hanging free.
Cut the mushroom cap in red felt and cut the window in pale blue. Stick into position, at a slight angle, with a scrap of lace each side for curtains. You can stitch equidistant threads of embroidery cotton up and down (double at the centre) and from side to side, 'darning' through the vertical threads.
Cut the window shape out again in another

Materials

Woven table mat or a piece of green fabric 18 inches by 12 inches.
Matching binding (for the fabric only)
2 thin garden canes about 14 inches long
$\frac{1}{2}$ yard narrow cord
Coloured felt squares
Braid, beads, buttons, flowers, lace, curtain ring, to trim
Black stranded embroidery thread
Fabric adhesive

Toadstool cottage

98

LEAF

colour for shutters, and then cut the piece in half. Snip a diamond shape out of each shutter as illustrated. Stick the shutters in position. Cut a window box in dark brown felt and fill it with lace and artificial flowers. Border the top curve of the window with broad braid. Cut different sized spots in cream felt and stick them at random over the red roof. Trace the chimney following the broken line and cut out in grey felt. Stick the chimney behind the roof.

Place the stalk and roof on the background fabric, the roof overlapping the stalk as shown, with the base of the stalk $3\frac{1}{4}$ inches from the bottom edge. Stick both pieces down firmly.

Cut the waterbutt and hanging basket in dark brown felt and trim the waterbutt with two bands of narrow braid. Stick both into position and embroider two threads to hang the basket from the roof.

Cut shapes in grey and beige felt for the path. Stick some green braid round the bottom of the stalk and dot gaily coloured flowers over the braid. Put a few flowers into the basket and arrange the rest over the foreground. Trace the leaf pattern from the diagram and cut out in green and gold felts. Stick a group of leaves in the upper corners of the hanging, as illustrated.

Finally, thread the canes through the channels at top and bottom to support the hanging. Knot the cord at the top.

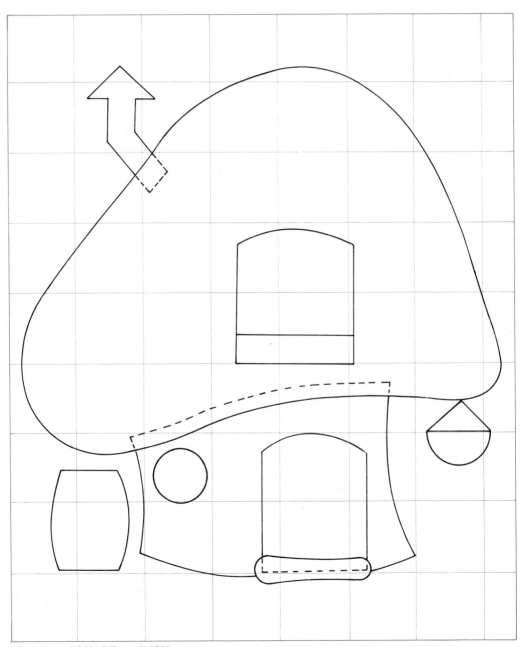

SCALE: 1 SQUARE=1 INCH

Boy's Tidy Bag

Hang these gay tidy bags in the children's rooms and perhaps pyjamas and nighties will disappear neatly inside each morning! The collage designs would make attractive circular pictures to match.

Method

To make the bag, turn and press a 4 inch hem onto the right side along each selvedge (see diagram). Stitch each end of the turning, taking $\frac{1}{2}$ inch seam, as indicated by dotted line. Fold the hessian in half along the line coloured on the diagram, right sides facing and join the side seams as far as the lower edge of the selvedge edge, finishing off very securely. Trim seams and turn bag and hems to right side.

Cut two pieces of pelmet buckram 12 inches by $3\frac{1}{2}$ inches and fit one inside each top hem. Fix buckram to the facing by glueing or catch selvedge neatly to the inside of the bag. Cut the piping in half, binding each end securely and stitch to the front and back with ends 6 inches apart, to form handles. To work the collage designs trace off and then cut each piece separately following the coloured line to complete the shape where indicated on the pattern. Follow the directions carefully for the order in which to work.

The Boy:
Cut the whole head, extending the neck as indicated by coloured line, in flesh felt: embroider the mouth in stem stitch and cut the eyes in black felt. Stick them into position. Cut the hair in brown felt and stick over the top of the head. Cut a circle of deep yellow felt for the hat, and stick this behind the head.

Materials

For each bag:

15 inches of 36 inch wide hessian
$\frac{3}{4}$ yard thick piping cord
Stiff pelmet buckram
Coloured felt squares
Broderie anglaise
Lace, ribbon, trimmings, as illustrated
1 yard lace or ric-rac braid
Red stranded embroidery thread
Black stranded embroidery thread
Fabric adhesive

Boy's tidy bag

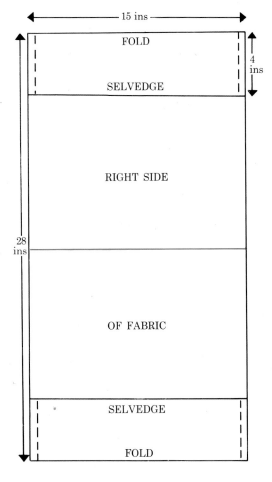

Cut the suit top in mid-blue felt, cutting the centre front opening level with the inside edges of the collar. Cut a rectangle of striped ribbon or fabric as indicated and stick this behind the suit top, as illustrated. Cut the two collar pieces in white felt and stick into position. Cut the hands in flesh felt and stick the wrists behind cuffs. Now stick this body over lower edge of neck, as pattern.

Cut the trousers in deep blue felt, extending the top edge and the legs as shown by coloured lines. Stick trousers behind the lower edge of the suit top. Cut the boots in black felt, and stick over the lower edges of the trousers.

Stick the whole figure to centre front of the bag. Surround the figure with a 9 inch diameter circle of ric-rac braid or other decorative trimming.

Girl's Tidy Bag

Method

To make the bag, see page 102.

To work the collage designs trace off and then cut each piece separately following the coloured line to complete the shape where indicated on the pattern. Follow the directions carefully for the order in which to work.

The Girl:
Cut a circle of flesh felt for the face: embroider the mouth with two straight stitches and cut the eyes in black felt and stick into position. Cut the hair in brown felt, following the coloured line indicating the lower edge, and then cutting up the vertical coloured line under the chin. This makes it easier to cut away the face section round the hairline. Stick hair over the face section. Cut the hair-bow and the bodice (to edge of face) in lilac felt: stick bow behind hair, and bodice over lower hair. Cut the sleeves and the whole skirt, in deep pink felt. Cut the hands in flesh, and stick behind cuffs as indicated. Cut the pinafore in broderie anglaise and stick over skirt. Trim the lower edge of the pinafore with white guipure lace, the neck and cuffs with white, and stick tiny coloured motifs over the sleeves. Stick coloured lace behind lower edge of skirt so that it is just visible below the hem. Cut the legs in black felt and stick behind skirt. Now assemble the upper and lower sections of the body and the two sleeves, and stick them to the centre front of the bag. Surround the figure with a 9 inch diameter circle of lace flowers or other decorative trimming.

Materials

For each bag:

15 inches of 36 inch wide hessian
¾ yard thick piping cord
Stiff pelmet buckram
Coloured felt squares
Broderie anglaise
Lace, ribbon, trimmings, as illustrated
1 yard lace or ric-rac braid
Red stranded embroidery thread
Black stranded embroidery thread
Fabric adhesive

Girl's tidy bag and owl and pussycat collage

Bathroom

Give a wicker wastepaper basket a new lease of life
with a pretty padded covering. For decoration, an
arrangement of dried flowers in an old-fashioned
glass storage jar looks most attractive.

Daisy Linen Basket

Underwear and stockings wait, ready for the washtub, in this flower-patterned linen basket. It is made from an inexpensive waste-paper basket but with a pretty padded top and wipe-clean lining, it has become a dainty bedroom or bathroom accessory.

The basket illustrated was 10 inches deep with a top 10 inches in diameter.

The directions given can be adapted to any size of basket.

Materials

Straw waste-paper basket
Plastic sheeting for lining
Fabric for lid
Wadding
Stiff cardboard
1½ yards of 1 inch wide frilled lace
Fabric adhesive

Method

Measure the depth, the outside top edge of the basket and the diameter of the base. Add 1½ inches to the measurements. Using these measurements, cut a strip of plastic for the sides and cut a circle for the base.

With right sides facing, join the two short edges of the plastic strip for the side seam. Turn the top edge over ¼ inch to the wrong side and tack. Run a gathering thread round the lower edge, distributing the gathers evenly round the circle. Draw up gathers to fit the circle cut for the base, and stitch into position right sides facing. Trim the seam, fit the lining into the basket. Bring the top edge of the lining over the edge of the basket and catch plastic into place invisibly.

For the lid, measure the diameter of the top basket and add 1 inch to the measurement. Cut two circles of fabric to this measurement. Then cut two circles of wadding and a circle of cardboard to the same diameter as the top of the basket. Stick a circle of wadding to each side of the cardboard.

Pin the lace frill to the right side of one fabric circle, the outer edge of the frill towards the centre of the circle. Stitch the frill ½ inch from the raw edge of the fabric

Daisy linen basket

110

(see diagram). Right sides facing, pin the two fabric circles together then stitch, following the stitching line of the frill. Leave room to fit the padded cardboard inside. Trim the seam, then turn to the right side and pin opening before slip-stitching into place. Gather remaining lace frill and draw up tightly, forming it into a rosette. Catch together underneath and stitch securely to the centre of the lid.

RIGHT
SIDE OF
FABRIC

Flower Shower

Instead of bath salts, fill an old-fashioned apothecary jar with dried everlasting flowers and foliage for the prettiest of bathroom decorations.

Method

Shape a piece of Plasticine into a small mound about 1 inch high and approximately 1½ inches across the base. Press shells into the Plasticine to cover the sides of the mound. Stand the jar behind the Plasticine mound so that you can judge the height of the flower display. Cut lengths of foliage, grass and oats. Press these into the top of the mound. Fill in the lower section with flower heads, pressing the stalks into the Plasticine firmly. When the arrangement is completed, make sure that the inside of the jar is quite dry and clean and then drop a little adhesive inside the jar. Pick up the flower arrangement carefully, holding it by the top and lower it on to the adhesive. Leave to dry.
Sprinkle a few silica gel crystals into the jar to prevent moisture forming and seal the top of the jar.

Materials

Glass storage jar, about 6 inches high
Everlasting flowers and foliage
Small sea shells
Plasticine, stone coloured or white
Clear all-purpose adhesive
Silica gel crystals (obtainable from chemists or drugstores)

Photograph on page 2

Sewing Materials

It is always difficult to keep sewing materials tidy.
The tape measure châtelaine is an unusual idea
for keeping all you kit together. For pins, make the
Easter bonnet pin-cushions. If you are a keen
knitter, you will need a knitting granny to look
after all your materials.

Tape measure châtelaine

Tape Measure Châtelaine

Here is an idea for a complete sewing kit, attached to the ends of a tape measure. Wear the tape measure around your neck while working and everything you need is conveniently to hand.

Try to find a tape measure that has a hole at each end or, if necessary, make the holes and finish them off with an eyelet.

Method

Pin cushion
Cut two 3 inch squares of contrasting felt for the pin cushion. Oversew together round three sides, stuff firmly and oversew the remaining side. Oversew back again in the opposite direction as before.

Thimble case
Cut two circles 2 inches in diameter from contrasting colour felt. Oversew round two-thirds of the circle as before. Stitch a press fastener inside the opening to close.

Thread holder
Cut two 2 inch squares of contrasting colour felt for the thread holder. Oversew two opposite sides as illustrated.

Scissors case
Trace the pattern for the scissors case from the outline given. Place your own scissors on the pattern and adjust the dimensions and adapt the shape as necessary. Cut the whole shape out of felt twice for the back and cut the front, lower section out once. Cut the back shape out again in buckram or cardboard, slightly smaller than the pattern. Stick the buckram lightly between the two back pieces and tack the front section into

Materials

Coloured felt squares
Trimmings
Buckram or cardboard
Filling
Narrow cord
Small press fastener
Fabric adhesive
Tape measure
Scissors
Thimble
Skein of assorted threads
Needles and pins

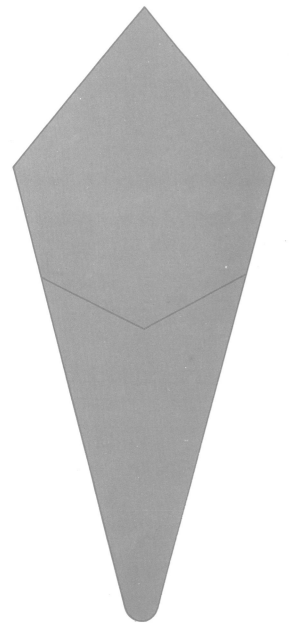

position. Oversew all round the edge with contrasting thread and then oversew back again in the opposite direction, crossing the first row of stitches.

To assemble the châtelaine, knot one end of the cord and stitch the knot to one corner of the pin cushion. Cut the cord off about three inches away, thread through the hole in the tape measure and knot the other end. Stitch the knot to the thimble case. Repeat with the scissors case and thread holder. Trim each item as illustrated.

Knitting Granny

Every busy woman needs a knitting granny. She looks after sock needles, crochet hooks, stitch holders . . . and all those other small items which tend to get lost at the bottom of the work basket.

You need a cardboard inner tube – and if you want your granny to hold full-length knitting needles, look for a longer tube!

Method

First close one end of the tube as follows. Cut a circle of cardboard the same diameter as the tube, and stick it to the centre of a circle of fabric about $\frac{3}{8}$ inch larger all round. Snip the excess fabric into tiny tabs all round, then place cardboard over end of tube and stick the tabs round the edge of the tube, to hold the end securely into position.

For the face, measure the circumference of the tube and add $\frac{1}{2}$ inch to the measurement. Cut a strip of flesh felt this length by 3 inches deep. Embroider the mouth in the centre, about $\frac{3}{4}$ inch above the lower edge. Stitch curtain rings above for spectacles with a bar across the centre. Stick or embroider a tiny circle of black felt in the centre of each line for eyes. Stick the felt round the top, open, end of the tube, level with the edge, ends overlapping at the back. Make a skein of wool (yarn) for the hair by winding grey double-knitting wool (knitting worsted) 20 times round an 8 inch deep piece of cardboard. Tie the loops at each end, slip off the cardboard and tie loosely in the centre. Catch the centre to the felt at front of tube, above the face, then take the sides round to the back and stitch firmly into position to cover the rest of the 'head'. Cut a piece of fabric to cover the remainder of the tube, and

Materials

Cardboard inner tube
Printed dress cotton
Flesh-coloured felt
Scrap of black felt or embroidery thread
White nylon net
Grey knitting wool (yarn)
Lace, ribbon, etc. to trim
2 × $\frac{1}{2}$ inch diameter curtain rings
Red stranded embroidery thread
1 cocktail stick
2 small wooden beads
Scrap of contrasting wool (yarn)
Narrow round hat elastic
Cardboard
Stiff paper
Small piece of foam sheet or a large cork
Fabric adhesive

Easter bonnet pin cushions and knitting granny

118

stick into position. To make the arms, trace
the pattern shape and cut out twice in stiff
paper. Cover one side of each arm with
fabric, cutting it level with each straight
edge, but leaving surplus along each side,
snipping it into tabs and sticking to the back
as for the base. Trace the hand and cut twice
in flesh felt, then stick a hand under the end
of each arm as indicated. Stick the top of each
arm level with the neck, then stick the
lower part to the body (leaving the hands
free), so that the elbow area stands away
from the body slightly.

Trim the neck, wrists and lower edge with
lace, ribbon and a flower as shown. Wind
coloured wool (yarn) into a small ball. Cut
the cocktail stick in half and fix a bead to
each blunt end: push points through the
wool (yarn), then place between granny's
hands. Stick securely into position.

Roll up a strip of foam – or use a large cork –
to close the open end of tube.

Cut a 9 inch diameter circle of double net for
the mob cap. Cut a 6 inch diameter circle of
paper and tack it to the centre of the double
net. Catch elastic to the net in a circle, just
outside the edge of the paper – use a running
stitch working alternately each side of the
elastic. Draw up the elastic to fit round the
top of the head.

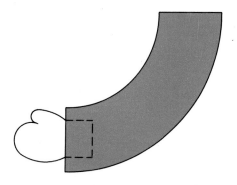

Easter Bonnet Pin Cushions

You may not find many occasions to *wear* anything quite so fancy as these pieces of millinery – but as pin-cushions, they will be in use all the time.

Method

Brown boater:
Cut two circles of felt 4 inches in diameter and a strip 8 inches long by 1 inch deep. Then cut a 2½ inch diameter circle from the centre of one large circle: this circle will form the top of the boater. Cut a piece of stiff cardboard slightly less than 4 inches in diameter. With tiny stitches, oversew one long edge of the side strip round the edge of the small top circle. Join the two short ends where they meet. Oversew the other edge of the side strip round the inner edge of the large circle from which the top was cut. Stuff the crown of the hat very firmly, then place the cardboard on top of the stuffing, with the second felt circle on top of that. Oversew together all round the outer edge of the brim. Catch lower edge of crown through to underside of brim, to hold the shape neatly. Trim with a band of narrow ribbon and a large daisy.

Green cocked hat:
Follow the instructions for the boater, but cut the side strip 1½ inches deep. Cut the card 2¼ inches in diameter. Fit the card inside over the stuffed crown.
Trim the outer edge of the brim with lace edging and catch it to the crown at each side. Trim with two flowers.

Violet toque:
Follow instructions given for making the boater, but cut the two circles 3 inches in diameter with a 2¼ inch diameter top circle. Cut an 8 inch side strip, 1½ inches deep. Cut card slightly less than 3 inches in diameter. Trim with 1¼ inch wide lace, gathering it into a wide bow at the back, and add a bunch of tiny forget-me-nots in front.

Materials

For one hat:
Piece of felt (about 8 inches by 6 inches)
Stiff cardboard
Filling
Flowers, ribbons, lace, beads etc. to trim
Fabric adhesive

Patio and Out-of-Doors

For outdoor parties, you can make very attractive candles, with decorated pottery bases. And, for cleaning the car, make the reversible chamois leather and sponge mitten.

Oriental candles and pottery candle bases

Oriental Candles

Candles with an expensive, hand-made look can cost as little as the cheapest plain variety – plus the cost of a packet of children's wax crayons. Be sure to buy good quality crayons; not only are the colours more subtle, the results are far more satisfactory.

Materials

Coloured crayons
A white candle

Method

The basic method is simple. Peel some of the paper covering from the crayon. Warm the end of the crayon in a flame and dab it on the surface of the white candle, rather as you would use sealing wax. Cover the whole surface of the candle with random spots of contrasting colour. Then fuse the crayon spots to the candle by partially melting it in the flame of a candle (although this gives a slightly blackened effect) or a gas flame. Move the candle slowly in the flame and allow the wax to melt sufficiently for the colours to run into each other.
Try decorating a plain purple candle with heavy blobs of gold crayon or cover the whole surface of a pale pink candle with spots of carnation pink and violet, running them into each other. Stripe the lower half of a blue candle with deep blue and green, fusing them together. The variations are endless – and great fun!

Pottery Candle Bases

These pretty candle holders are so simple to make that even children can learn to do it. They would enjoy the fun – and have results they can be proud of.

Method

Roll a lump of clay to about the size of a table tennis ball. Press it down on a smooth surface to make a firm, flat base. Press the base of a candle well down into the centre of the clay, so that it is firmly gripped. Shape the sides of the holder round it.

Remove the candle and gently smooth the surface of the clay all over with water, so that it is quite wet. If you want to incise a design or decorate the surface in any way, do so now. The rounded tip of a blunt cooking knife was pressed into the clay at random all over the outside of the gold candle holder. Leave the holder in a warm, but not hot, place to dry.

When quite dry and hard, paint it with poster colours, finishing with a coat of varnish, or use enamel.

Pink and purple poster paints were used for one of the candles illustrated, streaked blue poster paint over very wet green for another and gold enamel for the third.

Materials

Self-hardening modelling clay
Poster paints and clear varnish or enamel
    paints

125

Car Wash Mitten

Make this really practical reversible mitten for easy, efficient car cleaning. One side is made of foam sheeting and the other of chamois leather.

Method

Draw out the mitt pattern following the diagram measurements. Use a pair of compasses to draw the top curve, placing the point 4½ inches above the centre of the base line. Cut the mitt pattern once in chamois and three times in foam sheeting.
Place the chamois and matching foam shapes together and oversew the straight, wrist edge. Place the two contrasting pieces of foam together and oversew the wrist edge in the same way.
Place the two sides of the mitt together right sides facing, chamois inside, and oversew all round, stitching very securely at each wrist corner. Turn to right side.

Materials

8 inch square of chamois leather
3 × 8 inch squares of ¼ inch thick foam
sheeting (one to match the chamois, two in a contrasting colour)

Car wash mitten

126

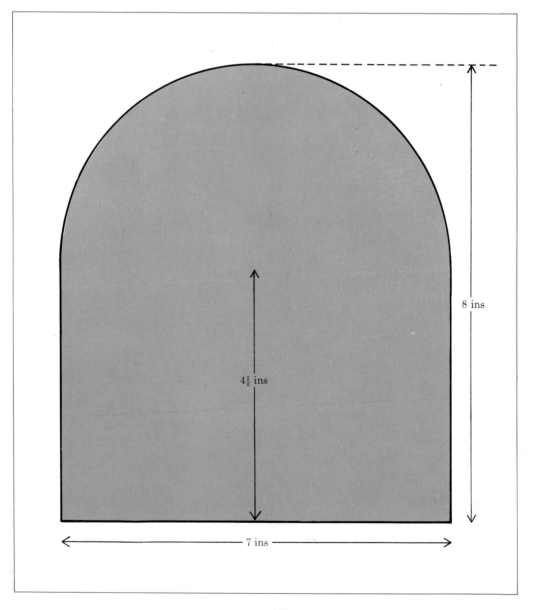